Grace
The Desire and Ability
to
CHANGE

OR

I Want to DANCE

By Lynndon (Lynn) Thomas

Table of Contents with Subsections

Dedicated to My Daughter

Reverend Micaiah Thomas Tanck

The Dancer

Introduction

Why do we seem powerless to change? Here is the good news: we can change. Sure, you say—isn't change a problem of motivation and ability? We just need to have the will and skills to change. But here is even better news: God can give us the motivation, the passion, and the ability to change. God can gift us both the desire and the ability to be different than we are.

You will learn from the fourth century Roman theologian named Augustine, from northern Africa, that change is possible. This famous Christian theologian changed the world when he explained grace. He clarified the idea that grace comes from the Holy Spirit, affecting our lives like a mighty wind. Grace changes us so that we desire what is pleasing to God. Augustine explained that it was possible to live righteously in ways that please God and not be miserable in well-doing. Sadly, some of his revolutionary ideas were ignored, and many were misplaced in time. Centuries of time and events will do that, and important ideas can be lost. We are going to rediscover those amazing concepts. We can live holy lives and live in freedom, living as we want to live. How? By grace.

Grace, The Desire and Ability to CHANGE, or I Want to DANCE, is the title of this book, after several other considerations. One title considered was *The History of Grace*. People, technology, countries, and even ideas have history. Although this book traces the history of the "concept" of grace from the fourth century to the present day, this book is more than a history book about grace. Another idea for a title was *Grace—The Power Within*. Grace has been explained throughout much of history as a force that heals by changing behaviors. I decided the book's contents more accurately reflected how to change. I also considered the title *Grace Misunderstood*. Sadly, the concept of grace was weakened because of theological battles in the church's history. As a result, its original classical meaning is unfamiliar to many Christians. This book takes us back in history and reveals a truth that was revolutionary and later obscured by excesses and controversies in the Church. As the result of the fog created by conflict in the church, grace was misunderstood, and there was confusion about salvation and transformation.

I landed on the title of this book because the bottom line is that grace can transform our lives like a stream of electricity can energize a motor. Grace is the force, the power that makes things happen in our lives. And it can be activated and used for change. If you are one of those who feel that things need to change but are uncertain how to change—well, grace is the answer.

Early in life, I was fortunate enough to hear grace defined in a helpful way. Someone said in a conference: grace is God in us, making us willing and able to do God's will. I later learned this was the classic and ancient definition of grace. As the years passed, I was perplexed why this classical understanding of grace as a force of change had been replaced with the idea of grace as a state of being. As I grew in my faith and later experienced God's call to be a minister and a missionary, my theological studies helped me understand how grace had been transformed from a force of change to a powerless concept. Starting churches and training leaders forced me to study and reflect. I became aware that many pastors and church leaders were unclear about what grace was. For many, grace was not a force of change; it was just a new understanding about oneself.

The common idea we hear is that by God's grace, God accepts people despite them being horrible people. Thus, grace is the reality that I am accepted. This is true. I am aware that God accepts me as a sinner. But grace is not acceptance; it is a force of change. The grace concept that I was taught, the classical understanding of grace, is that grace is transformative. Grace is making me different. In this context it functions as a verb, an action, a power. Grace is a force of change, and we can turn it on. Grace is not a one-time thing. It is a dynamic force that is changing us and guiding us. Grace is a continuous action. Grace, once ignited, produces a roaring fire of change. God accepts us, and we are undeserving, but that is not grace. Grace is much more; it is a wind that moves us to new places. It makes us different. Like a sailing ship riding the high seas, we ride on the winds of grace.

If grace is a force that changes us, a wind that moves us, then we need to understand it and know how to set our sails to catch the wind. What makes grace "amazing" is how we get it and how it changes and leads us. This book looks at the history of grace and how the early theologians interpreted the Bible and defined grace. I will draw from history to rediscover grace. Think of theologians as interpreters of scripture. They read God's word, think about it within their context and from their experience with God, and explain what those scriptures mean. You will hear from many different theologians in this book who come from many different backgrounds.

Chapter 1 looks at the motivational problem of change. To change, we must have a wind that pushes us to be different. We must have a will to change. In Chapter 2, we discover the ideas of the early theologians, which reveal a fresh understanding of what grace is and how we are changed. Grace goes to the heart of human desire. In Chapter 3, we will explore what grace looks like in the life of the Christian. Grace inspires love that leads to belonging. Chapter 4 will look at how grace and good works interact. Love involves virtuous works. Chapter 5 explores different views on where grace comes from and how it can be activated. We even look at grace from a scientific and psychological perspective. Chapter 6 looks at how to live a life that is constantly transformed by grace. Grace changes us by motivating new skills of likeability. Chapter 7 talks about how grace makes each of us a unique person and how it shows us God's will for our life. Grace gives us our personhood. Chapter 8 shares many passages from the Bible, explaining them in light of grace as a force of change in our lives. Chapter 8 may be the most exciting because it explains famous scriptures in the light of transformative grace. For some, this may be the first time these verses now make sense. Finally, the last chapter provides a conclusion and summary of the book. As you read this book, I believe you will have an amazing journey.

One of the fascinating aspects of the study of grace is how many theologians draw from Augustine to understand grace. Aurelius Augustine of Hippo (modern-day Annaba, Algeria) was a renowned early church leader. Outside of the Apostle Paul, Augustine probably had the most influence on foundational theology in the Roman Catholic Church and the Protestant Church. He is often referred to as the doctor of "grace." Many famous Roman Catholic and Protestant theologians were students of Augustine's ideas. The great Protestant Reformers, such as Luther and Calvin, were students of Augustinian theology and believed their Reformation ideas had their roots in Augustine. No classical theologian (Catholic or Protestant) disagrees with Augustine's understanding of grace as a healing force. Interestingly, many church reform movements, both Catholic and Protestant, can trace their roots to someone who was studying Augustine. By returning to Augustine and following the development of the theology of grace, I believe we can rediscover how to delight in change. That was Augustine's innovative idea: change can be delightful.

Theology tends to be abstract—that is, theology tends to be philosophical and not visual. This book uses the analogy of dancing to help visualize what grace does. My daughter was an accomplished ballerina for many years. I saw a great deal of dancing, and I saw how dancers developed and changed as they danced. After a few years, I could spot a ballerina just by how they moved and stood. Dance changed them. I also saw the community of dancers become friends and grow in love for each other as they danced. I realized that dancing produced change in each dancer. Their bodies changed, and they gained abilities as dancers. It also produced a community. Dancing was their way to belong and be accepted. They became a troupe of performers. It is my hope that by using dance as a visual illustration, you can understand the concepts. Above all, my goal is to show you a path to change, to spirituality, to godliness, and to freedom in Christ that is delightful. You can dance!

1. Change: Why I Cannot Dance

Never underestimate the human ability to live complacently in a bad situation.

Paul has always been fascinating to me. He first appears in the Bible (Acts 8) as a hateful religious fanatic. He is a Pharisee, passionate about the eradication of heretics. His method of bringing about religious purity is death by angry mob. I would like to take a moment to talk about Saul, Paul's evil alter ego.

Saul was a highly educated, religious man. He said this about himself (Galatians 1:14), and everyone confirmed he was a Pharisee of Pharisees (Acts 23:6). He was outspoken about his faith and so zealous that any threats to the purity of his Jewish faith were met with confrontation. Saul was not a soft-spoken and discreet believer. He willingly participated in death squads that hunted down Jewish heretics. As a result, he ran into Jewish followers of Jesus. These followers of Jesus, who were not at this time called Christians, were wayward Jews in the mind of Saul. Their removal from Jewish society was the only way to protect the true faith, in Saul's view. There was no room for diversity of thought in Saul's world. We first meet Saul in a bloodthirsty mob of zealots, as the mob was assassinating Stephen, a young Jesus follower (Acts 7 and 8). Stephen was stoned to death by a gang of men—a tortuous and public death designed to send a message.

The next encounter with Saul is the Damascus Road experience (Acts 9). The juxtaposition of these two stories highlights the magnitude of the Damascus Road story. Saul was traveling to Damascus to find and imprison more heretics. He was the Taliban of Judaism. There was a flash from heaven; he fell to the ground, was blinded, and heard a voice. The voice asked why he, Saul, was persecuting God, and the voice said to standby for more instructions. Saul was taken into Damascus. God spoke to a follower of Jesus that lived in Damascus named Ananias and told him to find Saul. Ironically, Ananias was probably one of the heretics Saul was sent to arrest. Saul found God on the road to Damascus, and Ananias helped explain what he had actually found. Saul had found Jesus Christ. Acts 9, 22, and 26 are three accounts of his dramatic conversion. And in Paul's letters, we see his explanation of his remarkable conversion to Christ. His new life went from darkness to light, from being an intolerant murderer to a loving apostle. Paul explained that he had been the chief of sinners, and the Bible records that he dramatically changed (1 Timothy 1:12-15). Saul was changed from a murderer of Christians to a Christian missionary. This book looks at change—how to be different than we are. If Paul's change could be so dramatic and swift, there is hope for all of us.

Nicodemus and The New Wind

The Roman Catholic priest Juan Luis Segundo (1973, 2:59–62) tells the story of Nicodemus in his book, *Grace and the Human Condition*. Nicodemus was a Pharisee and a member of the Sanhedrin. He was a respected and accomplished man of God. He was not like the other Pharisees. He was open-minded, kind, and willing to engage people he did not understand. We see him three times in the Gospel of John: in his first meeting with Jesus, his defense of Jesus before the Sanhedrin, and his participation in helping with Jesus's burial. He was certainly not like the Pharisee Saul, who was narrow-minded and hostile against any Jew that explored new ideas about Judaism.

Nicodemus approached Jesus one night to ask him who he was and what he was doing. Nicodemus stated that he knew Jesus was a teacher and was a man sent from God. He was there to gain a new perspective about God's Kingdom. The virtuous and godly Pharisee was about to have his world shaken. Jesus responded, "You must be born again" (John 3:3). Nicodemus was confused. Jesus clarified, "Unless one is born of water and the Spirit, he cannot enter the kingdom of God" (John 3:5). Nicodemus was there to ask about God's Kingdom, but Jesus's response did not fit into anything he had heard or studied. Keep in mind, Nicodemus was a good Pharisee; not only was he faithful and accomplished, but he was also a nice guy. He did not demand respect from Jesus or brag about who he was.

Nicodemus was looking for some pointers to be better, but Jesus said that he had to start all over. Jesus challenged the Pharisee to a new beginning. We later learn that Jesus means that the new start involves entering the new covenant. In other words, God transforms us. God, by His Spirit, is infused into us. Karl Rahner, a famous Catholic theologian, explains that by grace, we are "divinized" (Rahner 1961, I:299). Spiritual new birth is an entirely different existence, like being born all over again. We become different; we change. The essence of salvation is change. What drives this new existence?

Jesus had never been clearer about God's Kingdom: "The wind blows where it wishes, and you hear its sound, but you do not know where it comes from or where it goes. So it is with everyone who is born of the Spirit" (John 3:8). Segundo calls the grace experience the "new wind" (Segundo 1973, 2:59–60). The grace of God is the wind of God. It comes from God's Spirit, and it brings new life by birthing everything new. We are born into new desires, new passions, and new abilities. All these qualities come from God, and they are infused into the believer. Grace is the wind that moves us to be what we have never been. We are "born" again.

To Want to Change

Probably none of us are satisfied with who we are or the things we do. We wish we were kinder, more loving, selfless, compassionate. We wish we had more self-control, greater purity of thought, that we were better at managing our time, weight, money, words, anger, and emotions. We wish that we were more like Christ, more of a spiritual person. Desires often lead us astray and then crush us. We love wrong, and we act wrong, and we talk wrong. We know when we have messed up because our destructive appetites lead to broken relationships and pain. Our passions lead to conflict and loneliness. Our passions, which feed our behavior, feel like an addiction we cannot escape.

I have observed people who are energetic, optimistic, friendly, successful, and kind. How can I be like them? I notice the godly, how devoted they are. How can I be that way and not be miserable? A young man once told me that he could not be a Christian. He would be miserable, he stated. He laughed as he questioned why anyone would give up their happiness to be an unhappy Christian. He clarified that he loved to party and being a Christian would be dismal. He thought being a Christian was a life of denying oneself pleasure and being lonely. The question is, can we change and find change enjoyable? Can we be righteous and not live a monastic life of isolation? The fear that faith and pleasure are separate experiences causes many to question the value of faith. Is it possible to be different, loving, spiritual, modest, moral, and enthusiastic about being that way? Can I be happy and holy?

The organizational change theorist John Kotter (2012, 41) of Harvard Business School explains that one should never underestimate the human ability to live complacently in a bad situation. I have met people whose behavior leads to a life of misery. I wonder why they continue to live the dysfunctional way they do. Obviously, even the casual onlooker believes they need to change. I ask myself, "Why can't they change?" Kotter observes that it takes a crisis to find the motivation to make changes (2012, 43). As Kotter notes, motivation to change is the key to change. People may not like the way things are, but they do not want to change. That is Kotter's point: we continue to live in a bad situation because we are not motivated to be different. How can we find the motivation to change?

This book explores where to find the motivation to change and what change looks like. Change can be as pleasurable as being hungry and eating one's favorite meal. Kotter's approach to change, which was less pleasant, was to motivate change by force. The manager can threaten termination or announce the impending bankruptcy of the company if people do not change. Intimidation can motive a business to change. Being forced to be different is not a pleasurable way to be different. Besides, fulfilling the manager's vision may not result in success. That approach is like being a prisoner, and every day, one is forced to live a certain way. Can change be something one wants to do, as opposed to being forced to do? What can we change to find success and flourish in life? Regarding our faith walk, can change be the freedom to act in ways that are pleasing to God and enjoyable to us?

I want to live in freedom, as opposed to being obliged to live a certain way. As a Christian, I also want to live as God expects me to live, and I also want to enjoy the way I live. I agree with my young, partying friend; I do not want to live righteously and be miserable. I want righteousness to be a pleasurable activity, like fishing, gardening, playing with children, ice cream with friends, riding a horse, sunning at the beach, or dancing. What if I could be different, be like God expects me to be, and at the same time find peace and freedom being that way? That is the problem that grace came to solve.

The Perplexing Word "Grace"

The word grace is universally used in somber tones by Christians and non-Christians to illicit self-reflection and sincerity. The hymn "Amazing Grace" is so universal that even the non-religious use it to convey authenticity. If anything, this universal embrace of grace confuses what grace is. The casual use of the word "grace" is pervasive, and its meaning unclear. Grace is not a placid, calm bay; it is a roaring wind on the high seas. The Holy Spirit is a person, and grace is a force that comes from God's Spirit. It is a dynamic wind that moves us. Grace does things inside of us that changes us.

Language, say the linguists, is tricky. I can look a word up in a dictionary and have a partial understanding of the word. It is like looking at a house through a pipe: I can see some of the house, but I do not see all the house, and I certainly do not see the yard or community. A word has a meaning, but that meaning is not a simple definition. The word represents an idea, a message, a story that traveled over time and through cultures. In order to fully understand a word and its message, one needs to interpret the word. The idea of interpreting is explaining the meaning of a word, its message, its story, and its history within the hearer's context (Moreau, Greener, and Campbell 2014, 73–74).

For example, the word *rice* means something different to a European than to a Latin American. Rice is a staple in Latin America. It is eaten every day and often eaten in more than one meal during the day. Just this sentence puts *rice* in a different context for most European readers. Rice is not an occasional side dish; it is the foundation of most Latin American meals.

The story of the word *grace* begins in ancient Greece. The word *charis* initially was used to mean "delight," or "being delighted in something beautiful." The word suggests that something is pleasing, or something is desired. Grace is the attraction one feels in one's heart when one sees something amazing. The ancient Greeks also used the word to refer to the feeling of kindness that a person feels after receiving a nice gift. Similar to the Greeks, the early Romans explained that grace was the favor the gods feel toward their devotees. The worshippers give gifts to the gods, and the gods are pleased. You can see this concept in the Old Testament in Genesis 6:8. Noah stood out in a world of wickedness as a virtuous man. God felt favor, delight, and grace toward Noah, and decided to save him and his family. God delighted in Noah's virtuous life, although he was surrounded by wickedness. This feeling of delight is the Greek/Roman idea of grace. God is full of grace, but God also gifts humanity grace.

Once we experience God, we struggle to find words to explain our experience. The only words we have are those of our culture. Thus, we do the best we can with the words we have. The New Testament writers picked the Greek word *grace*, which in Greek is *charis (Χάρις)* as an important concept to explain God's involvement in the life of a Christian. In English, the words *charisma* and *charismatic* come from this Greek word. In both cases, the word has to do with enthusiasm or passion. Early Christians understood grace as an act of God's power. Grace was supernatural power that dwelt in Christians (Kittel and Friedrich 1974, IX:376). In general, grace was defined as heartfelt assistance from God (1974, IX:377).

The early Christians looked at the book of Exodus and translated the Hebrew texts in the Bible using the word *grace* to describe what the Egyptians felt about the Jews of the Exodus. The Egyptians gave the Jews gifts and money as they left (Exodus

3:21). The Jews were attractive (favored) in the Egyptians' eyes, and they wanted to help them. This motivation to give was understood as grace (1974, IX:379). In the case of Exodus, to find favor from someone and be given a gift from them is understood as experiencing grace. Something motivated them to give willingly, and that motivation was understood to be grace.

In Paul's New Testament writing, grace is a central concept. Salvation comes through grace (Romans 3:23-24). Grace is a transformative power from God (Romans 5:20-21). As you will see in the next chapter, grace is a power that addresses human motivation and human passions, and it produces good works by influencing desires (2 Corinthians 9:8) (1974, IX:396). Christians in the New Testament used the word *grace* from the Greek perspective. Grace was understood as a force that could change a person.

One of the problems with the word grace in English is— English. The origin of the English word *grace* is based on the Latin word *gratia* and not the Greek word *charis.* As a result, the word *grace* became associated with the ideas of "free" and "thanks." *Gratefulness* ("thanks") and *gratuity* ("gift" or "tip") are based on the Latin word *gratia. To say grace* refers to a mealtime prayer, and it means to say thanks for the meal.

The Jesuit priest and theologian Roger Haight (1979, 6–7) notes that there is confusion about the word *grace.* Over time there have been many different ideas woven into the word. Christians have lost its unique message. Grace has become a fuzzy feeling, a song, a lofty expectation that everything will work out. As one can see, even translating the word changes its meaning. Greek grace (*charis*) is passion, and Latin grace (*gratia*) is thankfulness. Grace is used among Christians to cover a large spectrum of ideas. In order to recover its meaning and to appreciate grace as God's power to change us, it is necessary to learn the meaning of the word as it was understood in the New Testament and interpreted by the early church. Thanks to the doctor of grace, Augustine, we can rediscover the power of grace.

Mercy and Grace

Before we talk about grace, we need to talk about mercy. Part of the confusion over grace is that the word *grace* is often used in place of *mercy*. Grace's modern understanding is God's undeserved acceptance. God loves those who do not deserve to be loved. God accepts sinners. Like a shadow that flows over a person, such is God's love. Grace is not a force in us; it is a force that flows over us. God accepts us. Grace is God's benevolent feeling of acceptance toward the sinner. These ideas better define mercy, not grace.

Augustine, the ancient theologian of North Africa, explained that mercy is God's intervention. God decided to intrude into humankind's sin problem, even though God was not invited by humankind, nor does humankind deserve God's intervention (Augustine 2011, 14). Augustine used Paul as an example. Paul persecuted the Church; he was an enemy of God and God's people. But God intervened into Paul's sinful nature and showed Paul mercy by giving Paul grace (Augustine 2011, 10). God accepted undeserving Paul (mercy), and then God gave him grace. Augustine clearly saw them as two different things.

The evangelical writer and speaker Chuck Swindoll is representative of the modern Protestant definition of grace. Swindoll says grace is "to extend favor or kindness to one who doesn't deserve it or can never earn it" (Swindoll 1990, 9). This idea of grace is very similar to the idea of mercy. Swindoll presents us with the idea of grace as mercy, which is being loved when being loved is not deserved. Another example of calling mercy "grace" is found in the *Integrated Theology* book by Lewis and Demarest (1996, 221). This systematic theology book says that grace is God's benevolent compassion, and mercy is God's compassion. One can see the confusion this interpretation creates. Is there any difference between benevolent compassion and compassion? Are there two types of love? Is grace a hyper-love and love a lesser love?

These interpretations of the word *grace* illustrate the shortcomings associated with defining grace with the definition of mercy. Essentially there is no difference: grace is understood to be underserved love, and mercy is also undeserved love.

Let us revisit Augustine's idea of mercy and God's intervention. Remember the story about Saul on the Damascus Road? God started it. God reached out to a murderer, an undeserving killer, and offered Himself to Saul. This intervention by God is classic mercy, motivated by love. The beam of light that hit Saul should have been a lightning bolt that vaporized Saul; that would have been justice. God overlooked Saul's murderous nature and evil life and showed him mercy. God did not make Saul pay for his sins (i.e., death). God spoke to Saul, a sinner and persecutor of the Church on the road to Damascus, showing Saul mercy. The act of reaching out to Saul, a sinner, and accepting Saul, a sinner, was an undeserved act of mercy. Saul did not deserve God's intervention.

After God's intervention, God gave Saul the gift of grace. The act of intervention, showing mercy, was different than the gift of grace God gave. Mercy was God's willingness to overlook Saul's sins and not punish him, but grace was God's power invested into Saul's heart to make him different. Mercy stopped God's punishment; grace transformed Saul's life. Grace was about changing Saul's life.

For example, let us say you are driving down the road and the police pull you over. The officer explains that you are speeding, and the fine will be $300. You say you are sorry, and the ticket is deserved. Then the officer says, "Well...I am going to let you go without a ticket." The point is that even though you deserve the ticket—you were speeding—the police officer shows you mercy and says that she will let you go without a ticket. This act of mercy corresponds with the idea of intervening in your sin. Justice demands a ticket; mercy intervenes and forgets the crime. Then the police officer does one more thing. "By the way," she adds, "the Fraternal Order of Police is going to give you $500,000 as a gift." Grace is the gift, and it flows after mercy, but it is not mercy. Mercy stops the speeder and does *not* show justice. Grace empowers the lawbreaker to be different. The response to grace is to accept the gift and its transformation. Grace goes beyond mercy. It is a gift that empowers and changes. Grace is transformative, it is for the future, and it is a force that changes the life of the receiver.

Jesus makes a couple of interesting references in the Gospel of Luke. These scriptures speak to God's mercy. Jesus's followers asked him about Jews who had been killed and whose blood had been mixed with pagan sacrifices. And in the same conversation, he was asked about the 18 Jews who died when the tower of Siloam accidentally fell on them (Luke 13:1–5). The point was to ask why bad things happen to God's chosen people. Jesus's response appears callous: "Do you think they were worse offenders than all the others who lived in Jerusalem?" Jesus's point was that all of us deserve to die for our sins. None of us should be here on this earth. We are all sinners and deserve punishment.

Jesus then tells a parable about a fig tree. A man plants a fig tree, and after a year, it had no figs. The owner tells him to cut it down. But the man, a vinedresser, responds that he wants to work with it and see if it will produce figs (Luke 13:6–9). The fact we are all here, when we are all sinners and deserve death, shows God's mercy. God is merciful and shows mercy by giving us time to repent and change.

All of humanity deserves to be punished, but God waits. God shows mercy by not punishing us. But God does not leave us in our sins. Mercy has a companion, and it is grace. Grace changes us. We, as Saul, deserve to be vaporized by a bolt of lightning. Mercy intervenes because it is patient and waits in the hope that we experience grace and that we bear fruit. Grace is about bearing fruit.

All Mercy and No Grace – A Dance-less World

Let us take a moment to think about mercy without grace. What if all we got from God was acceptance (mercy) but no power to change (grace)?

For the sake of having a visual image, let us say there is a world of domesticated unicorns and constant rainbows with no rain, and in that world, everyone dances. We can call this mythical world "Rainbow World." Dancing is enjoyable and transformative. In this special world, people dance. As they dance, they bond and form a community. The dancing produces meaningful friendships, and the dancers celebrate each other through dance. In this world, all live in peace and honor each other. Their dancing builds unity. In this Rainbow World of dancing, everyone has three things in their heart: they have a passion to dance, they know how to dance, and their dancing results in delight for each other. The big payoff in Rainbow World is being loved, accepted, belonging.

So, I show up in Rainbow World, and I see it is a great community. They say I must dance if I want to be in Rainbow World. In Rainbow World, dancing is who they are, as well as what they do. Dancing is relational, and it is how they belong. I explain that I do not want to dance. I do not know how to dance. I just want to belong—just accept me! I want to be accepted, but I will not dance.

If Rainbow World just accepts all who arrive, then there is no dancing. The healing and unifying effects of dancing are lost, and the community of love and belonging disappears. It ceases to exist. Rainbow World will soon look like all the other non-dancing worlds. Without the dance, there is no community and no means of belonging.

Does grace, defined as accepting the unacceptable, destroy Rainbow World by giving all the non-dancers acceptance as non-dancers? How can we have a community if no one dances? When mercy and grace are the same idea, there is only mercy. Mercy is accepting the unacceptable, and there is no second act, which is grace—the power to transform. In other words, mercy without the gift of grace leads to a dance-less world. God accepts (mercy), then God transforms (grace); by grace, we dance. Grace is dancing and it produces community. Chapter 2 explains what grace is, but without it, our lives are changeless.

Saul once hated Rainbow World and tried to kill its dancers. Mercy ignored what Saul said and his hateful deeds. He was ugly and offensive. Saul was not worthy of belonging in Rainbow World. Mercy forgot his past mistakes and offenses. But grace gave him a new heart and the desire and ability to dance. As the book of Acts and Paul's letters well attest, dance he did.

Listen to Paul's response: "What shall we say then? Are we to continue in sin that grace may abound?" (Romans 6:1). Are we to continue not to dance so that dancing is pervasive? "By no means" (Romans 6:2). In other words, that is crazy. "Where sin increased, grace abounded all the more" (Romans 5:20). Where there was no desire to dance, the God-given desire to dance became an explosive and obvious manifestation. Paul is referring to a changed life. Where sin increased, there was no change, but when grace came, people clearly changed. They danced.

Grace Inspires Us to Dance

Rainbow World is for dancers, and grace gives dancers the desire and the ability to dance. Grace does not give non-dancers an excuse not to dance. Because God loves humankind, God gifts grace, but grace is not God's love or mercy; grace is a supernatural power of healing. Grace is an expression of God's love and mercy. God intervenes when we do not deserve God's intervention (mercy). Then God offers transformation through grace. Grace is the gift that we do not deserve. Thank you, mercy!

Grace is the only way that we can become dancers and form a community. Love speaks of God's intent; God wants to be reconciled with us and prosper us. God wants us to love as God loves. Mercy is God opening the door. God accepts us despite our ugly lives. Grace is the gift we receive and a power within that changes us by healing our hearts. Grace is God in us, causing us to be enthusiastic about loving God and loving others.

Using the analogy of Rainbow World, let us explore a little deeper what this world is.

- First, dancing and being around other people are inseparable. Without others, there is no dance. No one dances alone. Love is not an experience found in isolation. Love requires relational interaction. So does dancing. Dancing produces community. I think you get the idea: dancing is a metaphor for loving.

- Second, each person in Rainbow World has the ability to dance. Each is unique and skilled in dancing. Rainbow World is not a ridged ballroom dance of conformity; it is a celebration of many ways to dance. In other words, each person has their personality and unique skills, giving each personalized skills to love each other. Rainbow World is a celebration of many dances, like a multicultural banquet of different foods. Love can flow from different cultures, personalities, men, women, parents, children, young and old. The greater the diversity, the greater the experience.
- Third, the desire and freedom one feels when dancing is what drives everything in Rainbow World. The dancing is not embarrassing. It is not forced. Dancing flows from the heart, and consequently, dancing brings the community together. Rainbow World is a community of people living in freedom, dancing in harmony. Love affirms and values others, and it is sacrificial. Love results in deep friendships and acceptance.
- Fourth, the desire and ability to dance shapes Rainbow World's very culture. Others say, "Those people—well, they can dance." Their community is a place of loving others, being loved by others, and belonging. Rainbow World is noticeable to others because of the love found among those in Rainbow World. The dancing has a purpose bigger than just dancing. It announces how dancing is God's nature and we should all dance. People see God when they see our love and when they see our community. God dances, we dance, and everyone notices.

So, will Rainbow World let me join them just for the sake of belonging? No, they explain, it is the dancing that causes us to belong. We celebrate life together and find harmony in the dance.

Those in Rainbow World are not trying to be mean. Rainbow World is like birds in a flock. If the bird cannot fly, there really is no way for the bird to belong to the flock. Flying is what birds do. By dancing, we belong. If we do not dance, we cannot belong. By loving, I belong. If I do not love, I cannot belong. God, by grace, makes me love as God loves. The passion of grace in our hearts is how God reveals love. It makes love real and tangible. Grace is God in us, revealing what love looks like. Grace provides the desire to dance and the ability to dance. The consequence is belonging.

⌘

In the next chapter, we will rediscover the concept of grace from the early Christian church. Grace was a big deal and framed what it meant for Christians to be converted. If mercy opens the door, then what does grace do? If God's Kingdom is all about dancing/loving, then grace is the key to passionately and freely dance/love.

2. The Force: The "Want" to Dance

Our hearts are flooded with new desires to live holy lives.

The science fiction *Star Wars* movies introduced the idea of "the Force." In those movies the universe had a magical force that some people could tap. Once they embodied the Force, it made them powerful. They could control matter, communicate across galaxies, fight with superhuman strength, and torture enemies by just concentrating on them. The *Star Wars* Force was a force used to control and subjugate others.

Grace is as dramatic, but it is a force with a much different purpose. Grace is a force from God we use to control ourselves, not others. After the Bible was canonized, the idea of grace was soon a significant concept in the early Christian Church. The theologians of the third and fourth centuries looked at the Bible and their converted lives and discovered some amazing ideas. They believed that grace changed the converted and caused Christians to be passionate for God and godliness.

God's attitude toward humans is love, and grace, motivated by God's love, meets a human need. Humans need to be reconciled (reunited) with God and each other. Grace is a God-given passion, a longing for deeds of reconciliation with God and others. The irony is that this passion is God-given, yet it feels like our own passion. Grace is a gift to humans from God.

Just Do Good!

Augustine spoke extensively about grace, and he explained how grace was a force in the heart of the Christian with transformative power. By grace, he believed, we could change, and by changing we can be reconciled. We can thank a British monk for inspiring some of Augustine's best theological concepts. Pelagius, a well-educated theologian, moved from his humble life in England (or Ireland) to Rome, the big city of power and commerce. Pelagius was appalled by the moral condition of Rome, in particular the laxity of professing Christians. He started to preach a message of self-discipline—specifically, that the Roman Christians needed to clean their lives up and live righteously. Pelagius believed humans were responsible for their behavior and had the ability to live moral and ethical lives. His point was that Christians could live holy lives if they only tried. In fact, said Pelagius, humans can obtain salvation through living holy lives. The Presbyterian pastor, R.C. Sproul, states, "For Pelagius and his followers responsibility always implies ability. If man has the moral responsibility to obey the law of God, he must also have the moral ability to do it" (Sproul 2005). Pelagius believed people could stop sinning—that is, they could break the bars of sin that imprisoned them. They only had to will themselves to be good. Just do good!

In one of Pelagius's letters to a Roman woman seeking deeper spirituality, Pelagius talked about godly habits, explaining that one must consider human nature's power. Human nature, he noted, is created by God and in the image of God. What God made is good. In fact, humankind's nature is a God-given weapon to fight off sin. God gave humankind the resolve to do good things. Then Pelagius pointed to famous people that were living righteous lives. They were not even Christians, but they freely willed themselves to live ethical lives. "Where did they get these good qualities, if not from the goodness of their nature" (Segundo 1973, 2:18)? He concluded that if non-Christians could live righteously, how much more could Christians live godly lives? Pelagius explained that with Christ and the help of grace, Christians had natural sanctity (Segundo 1973, 2:18). That means we are all born with the internal fortitude (human nature) to do good (sanctity).

This idea produced a theological fight and resulted in a bonanza of ideas about grace on the part of Augustine. In short, Augustine strongly disagreed. His attacks on Pelagius had two effects: one, the name Pelagius became a theological dirty word. Being called a Pelagianist, in the world of theology, is akin to being called a heretic. When theologians get upset with each other, that is what they call each other. And two, Augustine's reaction to Pelagius resulted in foundational theological concepts that impact the Church to this day. Augustine's response resulted in him being called the doctor of grace. Much of what we think about salvation came from Augustine's reaction to Pelagius.

Pelagius probably got Augustine's attention, in part because of their theological difference, but mostly because Pelagius blamed Augustine for the mess in Rome. Pelagius believed that one of the reasons for the moral decadence in Rome was Augustine's teachings. Pelagius blamed Augustine for giving the hard-partying Romans an excuse to party. Augustine reacted to Pelagius's criticism; he was probably defending himself from being blamed for the decadence of Rome as much as he was developing theology.

Augustine, Grace is a Force

In contrast to Pelagius, Augustine said that the will to sin is, in fact, our prison. The jailer is our will. We sin because we want to sin. On this point, Pelagius would agree with Augustine. Pelagius would say we should go to war with our will and command it to be holy. We should break the bars and escape. In other words, just grab the bars and break out of the jail. Even non-Christians do this. They know how to behave; it is part of their human nature.

Augustine would say, how can a jailer free himself if he is the one in jail? We cannot break out. Obviously, the imprisoned cannot break out by their own power. Augustine said trying to will oneself to righteousness would lead to defeat. No one could overcome their sinful will by willing it away. As Augustine explained, "Man is assisted by grace, in order that his will may not be uselessly commanded" (Augustine 2010, 15). His point was that a person could not tell themselves to be good; that was useless. A person cannot say, "Today I will be good," and then simply be good. In other words, a person cannot flip a switch in their head and "just be good."

God's approach to transformation is based on the reality that we do what we want to do. Augustine explained that grace was an internal force from God. And what grace did was give the believer delight in doing good. Grace changes our "wants" (our will). One of the dynamics of grace is that it heals by allowing a person to overcome sin (Nieuwenhove and Wawrykow 2010, loc. 79). God calls us to faith in Christ, and when we answer that call, said Augustine, our hearts are flooded with new desires to live holy lives (Haight 1979, 36). The will is transformed by grace, and the transformation is based on new passions. We will ourselves to righteousness because grace infects our will with a desire for godliness. Grace gives us pleasure in doing good. This understanding about grace was the exciting message I heard as a young man: grace is God in us making us willing. At that time, I had no idea of grace's ancient North African roots.

The major contrast between Augustine and Pelagius was Augustine's understanding that our salvation and sanctification (doing good) were totally dependent on God. It is God in us that makes us willing to live holy lives. Pelagius believed we could bend our will toward God. Augustine said that only through God can our will be bent. The force of grace is what bends our will. Augustine meant that grace is an internal force that changed a person's appetite, from desiring sin to desiring righteousness. In other words, one's prison is one's will to do what he or she wants to do. The way out of the prison is God given desires to be different. The will is the key to freedom from prison.

Pelagius believed human nature could will goodness by human effort. The non-Christians doing good was the proof. Augustine did not agree. The key, believed Augustine, was to change our desires, our "wants." Augustine believed that grace was from God, and it was not manmade. Grace was the solution to the will that imprisoned us; it freed the will to want good things. These new, God-gifted desires freed us to serve God and others simply because we wanted to serve them. Our new will desired godliness. The grace-driven will felt like freedom, and it guided the Christian by flooding the heart with godly appetites. Augustine agreed with Pelagius that the wayward Romans needed to change. But change was only possible by grace.

Ironically, when one looks at Pelagius's writing, one sees strong evidence of Augustine's concept of grace. Pelagius said, "For I tell you that there exists in our souls what we might call natural sanctity" (Segundo 1973, 2:18). So far, this implies human nature trying to be righteous by human effort, but then Pelagius adds, "It presides over the temple of the soul, judging good and evil. It fosters good and upright acts and condemns evil deeds. And it judges everything as if it were a law within in accordance with the testimony of conscience" (Segundo 1973, 2:18). If one were to replace the term "natural sanctity" with the word grace, one would see that Pelagius just described Augustine's idea of grace. Pelagius saw grace and described it, but he was misinterpreting it as something arising out of human effort. In a moment, you will see why he misunderstood what he saw.

Grace is a power within, from God, that changes our will and fosters good and upright acts. It could simply be that these two theologians had the same transformative experience, and they were trying to understand it. But even if the experience was the same, their interpretation of the experience was different. Pelagius thought that the passion for doing good came from his own heart. If Augustine and Pelagius had been on speaking terms, Augustine might have been able to explain that those passions were from God and felt exactly like grace should feel—that is, one feels free, like it is their own passion. The beauty of Augustinian grace is that righteousness feels like freedom.

Pelagius's faith and piety felt like freedom. He thought it was he, Pelagius, who was acting righteously. Augustine would have told him, "No, it is God in you through grace changing your will." Pelagius was unknowingly pointing out one of the characteristics of grace. Grace from God feels like free will.

Augustine (2011, 55) describes the process of salvation and righteousness as follows: the Law produces awareness of sin, faith in Christ attains grace, and grace heals the soul so that it wills godliness. Through grace, the soul experiences the freedom to decide, and this freedom accomplishes the law. Righteousness is the freedom to do things we should do and not do things we should not do. The saved are free not to lust, not to hate, not to steal, and not to worry. The saved are free to worship, pray, read scripture, serve others, be humble, show kindness, and be peacemakers. This means that the way to right living involves new desires that are experienced as freedom. Those desires motivate us to righteous acts and attitudes, allowing us to form a relationship with God and others. I think you are starting to understand the idea: by grace, we dance. Why? Because we want to dance. We know how to dance. Thus, we dance in freedom.

The To-Do List

The Law outlines God's expectations of behavior. It is like a parent posting on the refrigerator door the list of chores the children are expected to do on Saturday. The prison is a lack of will to meet those expectations—to do those chores. This is Paul's point in Romans 3:22; the law explains righteousness. It is the list of expectations on the refrigerator door. But Paul goes on to explain that it is by faith that we can uphold the law (Romans 3:31). God does not destroy the list of expectations because the child says he or she does not want to do the chores. God, using the response of our faith, infuses grace into our hearts to free us from our apathy and disinterest. Paul explains that sin is no longer our prison because we are now under grace (Romans 6:14). Apathy is our prison, and we are powerless to do what we know we are supposed to do. Our prison, in other words, is that we do not want to.

If I, as a parent, had an energy drink that resulted in happy obedience to do the chore list, I would certainly give it to my cranky children on Saturday morning. Think of grace as that energy drink. Grace is a force from God, a medicine that gives godly passions and motivations. Grace changes a person's will, such that the person wants to meet God's expectations. God's will becomes the will of the person, and it floods the heart with new desires. This passion feels like freedom. Performing acts of righteousness is an expression of our freedom, not legalism. We fulfill God's expectations based on desire, not obligation. Through faith and grace, our will is re-born by new desires to please God. Jesus explained that this is the covenant of grace. Both covenants were focused on meeting God's expectations; the one that comes from Christ and the Holy Spirit makes that possible.[1] It is a mighty wind.

Because of the energy drink I give my apathetic children, they snatch the list from the refrigerator door and joyously do their chores. One could ask my children, "Who made you do these chores?" They would look confused and answer, "No one—we want to do these chores." It would be like asking children playing with the garden hose on a hot day, "Who made you play in the water?" What a crazy question! "We love playing in the water on a hot day," they would reply.

To force me to do what I do not want is legalism, and it has a short shelf life. I know what I should do, but I just do not want to do it. Paul explains that God has made known to us God's expectations. God's expectations are good, and they build community. But we have no desire to meet God's expectations (Romans 7:15-20). And as a result, we miss out on a loving community.

Let us go back to Rainbow World and see how this looks. If I want to get into Rainbow World, I must force myself to do what I do not want to do: dance. Anybody can fake dance; they can even fake that they like dancing. But fake dancing means that the very moment one can stop dancing, they will. It also means that one has two lives—a secret, non-dance life and a public, fake-dance life. And when one confides in others, he or she will cast doubts on dancing.

---

[1] Covenant theology consists of the concept of an Old and New Testament covenant. The Jews of the Old Testament were under the old covenant. They were expected to obey God's law. They used sacrifices to gain atonement for their sins. The Old Testament covenant is often called the covenant of works. The New Testament covenant is called the covenant of grace. Through the death and resurrection of Jesus Christ and grace from the Holy Spirit, the believer is redeemed (G. R. Lewis and Demarest 1996, vol. 3, pp. 208–09).

This is why the law fails us. It only tells us we should dance, but it does not help us dance. It sets us up to be hypocrites and deceptive. A lack of desire to follow the law causes us to reinterpret the law, lowering the standards, and even ignoring the law as irrelevant. The law is an obligation, a burden. As a result, we resent the law and try to find ways around it.

Hypocrisy was what Pelagius was seeing in Rome. Everyone said that they were dancers, but no one liked to dance. Augustine, reacting to Pelagius, observed that the unruly Romans would never be authentic Christians if they had to force themselves to do what they had no desire to do.

Augustine explained that righteousness based on grace worked, and righteousness based on human effort did not work. Workable righteousness was grace born from faith. God clearly revealed to humankind God's expectations, and God empowered humans by changing their will to fulfill those expectations. Righteousness was obtainable by God's divine assistance. Grace was understood to be an experience of freedom that God gave. God gave desires to the hearts of Christians. Freedom was doing what one wanted to do. Augustine railed against the idea that human effort could produce righteousness. Sinners could not will themselves to act righteously. Humans could not change under their own power.

To Pelagius's credit, he realized that righteousness should be part of the Christian life. He was critical of people who professed to be Christians but behaved in a manner that was not consistent with scripture. He did not reinterpret scripture to justify their poor behavior. He believed to be righteous, a person had to change. But what he was missing was the idea that grace combines freedom and righteousness. Pelagius was experiencing grace in his own life; he just misunderstood it. One of the dynamics of grace is that it produces the feeling of freedom, which can be mistaken as one's own human will. Grace is a God-given divine will.

Augustine said that to will oneself to dance would never work. Augustine's solution was the idea that a person must be re-programmed, and the way for that to happen is faith in Christ. Faith brings God's Spirit and grace from God. Grace is the wind that gives the person the will and ability to dance. The sailing ship moves, not by its own power, but by an external power. Paul said we were saved by grace through faith. Augustine (2010, 50) cites Philippians 2:13: "For it is God who works in you, both to will and to work for his good pleasure." We can do nothing without God working in us so that we will what God wills.

The only way to dance is to have the heart of a dancer. Grace puts that heart in us. The new heart, God's Spirit, is the wind that changes us. We join Rainbow World because we want to dance, and we have the gifted ability to dance. Therefore, we are dancers. As Augustine noted, grace heals us. We meet all the criteria of Rainbow World through grace. The passion for dancing is our salvation, and it comes through faith in Christ. Grace makes our dancing unforced and not legalistic. Paul puts it this way: "But if it is by grace, it is no longer on the basis of works; otherwise grace would no longer be grace" (Romans 11:6). Our dancing is from passion, and it is not forced; otherwise, the passion would not be passion. The only way to dance is to do so because we want to dance. The beauty of Rainbow World is that everyone dances, and they do so freely. Dancing is not an obligation. The passion comes from God, as does the knowledge of how to dance, and the dance creates a community.

Augustine understood sin as a problem of human will. As sinners, we addictively make ourselves the focus of our lives. Our values and norms all revolve around what is in our best interest. The remedy, believed Augustine, was a dose of grace. Roger

Haight (1979, 48–49), a theologian, believed that Augustine looked at salvation and righteousness from a psychological perspective. Grace is a healing force in the soul, allowing the Christian to love pleasing God and to love others, thus freeing the Christian from the bondage of selfishness.

Augustine's battle with Pelagius resulted in a new understanding about God's Kingdom and how it works. The Church began to build on this concept. The leaders of the Reformation, more than 1,500 years after Augustine, found his ideas to be profound. As a result, Protestantism and Reformed Theology were heavily influenced by Augustine.

Aquinas, Grace and Identity

One of Augustine's admirers was Thomas Aquinas. Aquinas was an Italian priest and philosopher, and he studied Augustine's writings. He lived about 800 years after Augustine, in the thirteenth century. Aquinas took Augustine's ideas of grace and explained them, often better than Augustine.

Aquinas expanded on Augustine's ideas. He agreed with Augustine on the point that grace is a God-given desire and ability to please God. But Aquinas took grace one step further. For Aquinas, grace was more than a psychological experience; it fundamentally changed one's nature (Haight 1979, 61–63). Nature has to do with tendencies. For example, human nature tends to be self-centered, selfish, and self-seeking.

Rik Van Nieuwenhove and Joseph Wawrykow (2010, loc. 31-33), both theology professors, explain that Aquinas divided the natural from the supernatural. Doing what one has the natural capacity to do is living within one's nature. Living outside of one's natural capacity is supernatural. For example, a squirrel can spring from tree limb to tree limb; acrobatic agility is in its nature. But a squirrel cannot enter a discussion with humans; that is not in its nature. Squirrels can do all kinds of squirrel things consistent with their squirrel capability. Therefore, our nature is a limitation. There are things we as humans cannot do. Selfishness is our human nature, and humility and selflessness are beyond our nature.

For Aquinas, our nature is what we are (Nieuwenhove and Wawrykow 2010, 27). We are humans that fulfill our human nature. As Paul explained, we humans have natural desires, but they are not pleasing to God (Galatians 5:17). The way we behave is offensive to God. Our natural behavior destroys communion with God and others. Aquinas explained that by grace, a person can rise above their natural human behaviors. They are changed into something different. Grace produces virtuous behaviors, and by grace, we obtain a supernatural state of being. Our virtuous nature (supernatural) becomes our new identity (Nieuwenhove and Wawrykow 2010, loc. 57). It is like the transformation of a caterpillar into a butterfly. The nature of being a worm is replaced with a new identity—that of a butterfly. Aquinas linked behavior and identity. His contribution to the idea of grace was grace gives us a new identity.

Augustine, in contrast, understands grace as a solution to a problem. For Augustine, humans are sick, and grace brings healing. It changes their hearts and behaviors. Human nature is sinful, and grace wages war against human nature through new passions and desires to be godly (Haight 1979, 57). Think of Augustine in this way: if human passions are driving sinful actions, then grace fights on the same battlefield by molding godly desires and passions. Godly passions, gifted by God to Christians, go to war against human passions. Augustine did not focus on a new nature (that is, a new identity). Augustine focused on change, on doing, not so much being a butterfly. His focus was on how grace bends one's will to godliness. To return to our metaphor, Aquinas focused on the dancer; Augustine focused on the dancing. It may sound trite, but an emphasis on the identity as dancer, and not the dancing, shifts one's priorities. What if you proclaimed that you had a title without the skills to back up that title?

What Aquinas did was connect dancing and dancer to the idea of grace. He added a new layer to grace, which was identity. Aquinas saw the healing aspect of grace, which Augustine had presented, but Aquinas added more. Aquinas explained that grace heals and elevates a person to a new nature, a new identity (Nieuwenhove and Wawrykow 2010, loc. 90-99). The Christian, a new being, is now pleasing to God because they are supernaturally inclined to be good (Nieuwenhove and Wawrykow 2010, loc. 108). Grace makes us a supernatural person. In the case of grace, explained Aquinas, we are dancers because God declares we are dancers. And what God declares, God creates (2010, loc. 171). We are dancers who are gifted the supernatural ability to dance.

This understanding is the basis of predestination. God selects some people to be saved. God gives select people a righteous identity, and then God gives the saved a desire to fulfill that identity (Nieuwenhove and Wawrykow 2010, loc. 241). God proclaimed our identity; we are dancers. Therefore, God empowers the saved to dance. From Aquinas's perspective, God creates our identity by the gift of grace. Then God gifts us grace giving us the desire and ability to dance, that is, to fulfill that identity.

If one has a dancer's identity but does not dance, one has a title and no skills. That person could be a "dance-less dancer." Is that possible? Aquinas and Augustine would say no. Aquinas was attempting to add more understanding about grace, not separate grace from virtuous behaviors or excuse bad behavior. However, by framing the idea of grace around both the dancing and the dancer, Aquinas opened the door to the temptation that someone would separate the dancing from the dancer. Now it is possible to confer titles to people who have no skills. We will talk more about that later.

Another innovation of Aquinas was to present two sides to the concept of grace. One side was the ability of grace to save (justification), and the other was the ability of grace to continuously produce new behaviors (sanctification). The term used for saving grace was "actual" grace (Pohle 1909b). The term used for the grace that impassions Christians to greater maturity, to live the virtuous life, was "habitual" or " sanctifying" grace (Haight 1979, 61). In other words, Aquinas saw two aspects of grace: the new identity of the converted and the passion for growing and maturing over time in one's faith.

Grace is like a waterfall; it cascades down the side of a mountain and continues its flow down the river. Grace is both a dramatic waterfall crest, "justification" (salvation), and a continually flowing river, "sanctification" (good deeds). The grace that produces conversion is the same grace that guides conversion.

Augustine's starting point is God gives us the desire to dance, and those desires change us. They make us dance. We are dancers because we dance. Aquinas (1991, 312–13 I-II, 110, #2), in contrast, says God gives us a new nature, a new identity, and we fulfill that identity via grace. Think of this as an issue of sequence. Augustine says grace produces godly passion and ability, resulting in godliness. If it looks like a duck, walks like a duck, and quacks, it must be a duck. Aquinas, in contrast, says God declares one godly, and the supernatural passion and ability quickly follow. First, God declares you are a duck, and then God empowers the duck to act like a duck.

Augustine, who lived about 800 years before Aquinas, focused on dancing—i.e., the act of dancing. For Augustine, dancing is transformative. By grace, we dance! Based on Aquinas, we would say that the nature of the people in Rainbow World is that they are dancers. God willed that they be dancers, and God made them able, through grace, to dance. God determines one's status, and grace helps one fulfill that status (Haight 1979, 56–61). When one separates identity and behavior, which was never Aquinas's idea, it creates a mess.

We Have to Go Back to Dancing

So, what is the big deal? These ideas seem to be terribly philosophical and abstract. I contend that, even if we do not fully understand it, grace is a big deal. It impacts our daily lives. How well we live our lives is directly related to grace.

If one separates dancing from being a dancer it creates a terrible imbalance and results in confusion about salvation and works. I believe we must go back to Augustine to regain the balance and appreciate what grace can do. As one looks at the development of theology over the centuries, especially in the Protestant church, one sees that the "identity" side of grace became the dominant understanding of grace—hence the imbalance. Separating identity from righteous works was never Augustine or Aquinas's idea of grace. Protestants know that Christians need to live holy lives, but they have found it frustrating to explain why because of the separation of identity and works.

Paul clearly explains that God has expectations, yet humankind cannot fulfill those expectations (Romans 2:12-16). Jesus also states the relevance of God's expectations related to behavior; Jesus did not come to abolish God's expectations for humanity (Matthew 15:17). In fact, in the Sermon on The Mount

(Matthew 5 and 6), Jesus said that God's expectations for human behavior are even higher than what is expressed in the Old Testament. For example, Jesus said, "You have heard we should not murder. I say you should not insult or hate others, which is the same as murder" (paraphrase). Jesus lists many Old Testament laws in his Sermon and then adds even higher expectations for fulfilling those laws.

Remarkably, grace can propel a person to the highest ideals of Christ. We cannot have community if we cannot live by behaviors that create community. And we cannot have those behaviors without grace. By grace we can love as Christ expects us to love.

Going back to Augustine, in Rainbow World, the dancers desire to dance. God gives them the desire. Grace is why they dance, and it is an experience of God's freedom. Through the dance, they are reborn as social beings. The dancing creates a community of acceptance and belonging. By going back to Augustine's ideas on grace, we are reminded that the key to communion is dancing. There is no other way to be called a dancer unless you dance. Augustine, who never talked about grace as an identity, understood grace as an action. Grace is "changing" us into the likeness of Christ. As Paul explained to the believers of the early church, "Continue to work out your salvation with fear and trembling, for it is God who works in you to will and to act in order to fulfill his good purpose" (Philippians 2:11-12).

⌘

In the next chapter, we will look at what righteousness looks like. What is it that grace is pushing us to do? If changing us is God's goal, then what should we change into? What does righteousness look like?

3. Love: The Dance We Are to Dance
We can love because grace inspires acts of love.

When we say that the people in Rainbow World dance, it is hard to visualize what that looks like. It is hard to visualize a new experience when it has never been part of our experience. When someone tells us about Rainbow World and its dancers, if we have never experienced Rainbow World, we can only compare it to what we know. This confusion is the challenge of crossing cultures. We interpret a culture that is new to us based on our own culture. As a result, we often misinterpret the new culture. Things in the new world can be so different from our experience that the only way to understand is by experiencing the new thing. This reality helps explain the challenge that non-Christians have in trying to understand God's Kingdom. They visualize God's Kingdom based on what they have experienced in their lives.

To know a new culture, one must be immersed in the new culture. This experience is like a missionary who becomes immersed in a different language, customs, norms, and worldviews. By cultural immersion, they understand those of that culture.

The illustration of Rainbow World has already provoked your imagination. As is the custom of most people, you likely reflected on your past dance experiences. Rainbow World is not like any dance experience you ever had. So, what does the dance in Rainbow World look like? Is there anywhere we can go to see Rainbow World?

The Basis of the Virtuous Life

Christianity, as well as most religions and cultures, has ethical standards. There are expectations as to how we are to behave. In the case of Christianity, one obvious source for guidelines on appropriate behavior is the Ten Commandments. We are not to murder, steal, commit adultery, lie, or swindle other people's property (Exodus 20). The Old Testament expands God's expectations to include dietary regulations, community health rules, policies about justice, regulations on property ownership, rules about human sexuality, and laws on marriage, to name just some of the general areas (see Leviticus). The New Testament also has behavioral expectations. Both Jesus and Paul, often referencing Old Testament concepts, clearly lay out expectations. Jesus's Sermon on the Mount is a list of dos and don'ts. Jesus's parables and interactions with others often lead to a behavioral expectation. Paul talks about fruits of the Spirit, which are Christian behaviors. Christians are to be kind, self-controlled (Galatians 5:22-23), flee sexual immorality (1 Corinthians 6:18), not steal, covet, get drunk, deceive others, worship idols, fornicate or commit adultery (1 Corinthians 6:9-10). There are many lists of expectations in the New Testament. Obviously, there are a great many expectations for Christian behavior. The question is this: what is the intent of all these expectations?

Both Jesus and Paul help us understand the foundation of these expectations. Jesus, when asked to prioritize the Ten Commandments, said there really are only two commandments. When asked about the Commandments, Jesus answered,

> The most important is, "Hear, O Israel: The Lord our God, the Lord is one. And you shall love the Lord your God with all your heart and with all your soul and with all your mind and with all your strength." The second is this: "You shall love your neighbor as

yourself." There is no other commandment greater than these.
(Mark 12:29-31)

Later Jesus said, "A new commandment I give you, that you love one another: just as I have loved you, you also are to love one another" (John 13:34). Paul said the same in Romans 13:9: he provided all the "thou shalt nots" and then concluded, "And any other commandment, are summed up in this word: 'You will love your neighbor as yourself'." So, what is the dance we are to dance? The dance consists of attitudes and actions of sacrifice and humility that demonstrate love. The intent of God's expectations is that we form a loving community by our behaviors.

In Jesus's long prayer in the Gospel of John (Chapter 17), before he left his disciples, Jesus explained God's Kingdom again. The prayer is full of relational words. The Vietnamese theologian Van Nam Kim says that to understand the prayer, one must read it from a sociological perspective (the group) and not a psychological perspective (the individual). God is "in" Christ, and Christ is "in" us (Kim 2014, 49–51). There is an inner dwelling, a oneness that the Father, Son, and Holy Spirit have, and Jesus desires that we also have this oneness with God and each other. The idea presented in the Gospel of John is intimacy. We are accepted and belong to each other.

The basis of God's Kingdom is the Trinity. Before creation, God was three persons, loving and being loved. As Augustine explained, "There is no love where nothing is loved" (Augustine 2014, 195). Love never takes place in solitude; it requires relationships. As the theologian Tim Chester explains, because God is in a trinitarian relationship, God is social and thus knowable. Chester's logic is that God knows God's self, and then God is perceived by others. Chester (2005, 136) states this as follows: "God is knowable because he is relational and he is relational because he exists as three persons in relationship." God is love because God is loving and loved, even before creation.

We can say that God started Rainbow World, and it was based on loving and being loved. As the scriptures illustrate, the Father loves the Son (Mathew 3:16-17, John 10:17), the Son loves the Father (Luke 22:42, John 17:4), and the Holy Spirit loves the Son and the Father (Luke 1:35, John 16:13-14). Their love is expressed through sacrifice and humility. Love for each other creates a community of inner dwelling, of oneness, of deep relational communion—each person is accepted and belongs. God's Kingdom is a community of love for each other. And love involves concrete actions called virtues. God is love; thus, God has to be virtuous. Rainbow World is virtuous. It must be if there is to be any love.

The Dance of The Trinity

The three persons of the Godhead do not co-exist alongside each other; they exist in inter-relatedness (Johnson 2002, loc. 595). The love between the Father, Son, and Holy Spirit is so deep and selfless that to know one is to know them all. Their love makes them one. Each person is unique yet indistinguishably identical in what they are: One God (Artemi 2017, 22). The American theologian Richard Gaillardetz (2008, 35) explains that God is loving and unifying, which means God's nature is to gather the different and, through the diversity, realize a new whole. Therefore, the new unity is diversity in communion. The Holy Spirit working within our hearts does not erase our distinctions and differences; in reality, the Spirit makes them non-divisive (Gaillardetz 2008, 38). Rainbow World is remarkable because there is diversity and, at the same time, acceptance and belonging. The only way that can happen is through dancing, meaning new behaviors that come from changed lives.

In the case of Rainbow World, unity does not take away each participant's uniqueness. Instead, by diversity in communion, it defines their personhood and unique mission. Think of this as a buffet of international foods. The diversity of different foods from around the world highlights the uniqueness of each dish. The diversity of foods is all the more beautiful because of their different tastes and textures. Rainbow World is remarkable because it involves love and diversity. This reality is why it is so energetic and fascinating. Grace inspires us to love others, even people that are culturally, racially, chronologically, and/or socially different than we are. And within our culture, race, age and gender we realize that our personalities, skills and talents are different, yet we love each other.

The diversity of the group and the glorification of each other is possible through the attitude of selflessness and the application of virtues. This is our example: the Father honors the Son, the Son honors the Father, and the Holy Spirit births the Church to honor the Son. Their selflessness towards each other makes them one, yet in three unique persons. Augustine (2014, 147) explains that the Father, Son, and Holy Spirit are of the same substance, and that substance is love.

Individualism and personhood are not the same thing. Individualism focuses on our agendas—those things that are our priority. Personhood speaks to being who we are in our uniqueness. Our uniqueness becomes a focus of praise. "This is my beloved Son, with whom I am well pleased" (Matthew 3:17). Trinitarian love is expressed as honor and praise for the other person, thus revealing each's personhood. As we honor each other, others know us. People know us as unique because others praise and honor us.

Love results in revelation; we are known because of love. Love requires that persons be in fellowship; love is not solitary. Individuals find agreement, even friendship, which results in praise and honor that reveals each person in the community. We are truly known because of the honor others give to us. As humans, we can achieve a level of intimacy, but not to the extent of the Godhead. Our love reveals each other as special, just as God's love revealed the fullness of the Persons found in the Trinity.

In contrast to humans, the Trinity is intensely sacrificial and always working for the honor and glory of the other. The concept is that all three persons of the Trinity mutually share in the life of the others. They are one. They are not individuals or detached from each other's actions (McGrath 1995, 404). Humans are only a shadow of trinitarian unity. However, the Holy Spirit in the heart of the Christian inspires him or her to honor and glorify others.

Through faith and grace, Christians, although imperfect in their attempt at community, are drawn to love, acceptance, and belonging. We dance the best we can, but we want to dance. We can love because grace inspires acts of love.

Rainbow World is a community, and grace pulls us into the community, helping us act in ways that build the community. The Trinity is our model for the giving of praise and honor to the Other. Loving communion is what Rainbow World is to be. The service and sacrifice seen in the Trinity is our challenge to serve, honor and sacrifice for others. The first Rainbow World was God's community, and it was the Father, Son, and Holy Spirit. God danced.

Shalom

The *Star Trek* TV series and movies introduced us to the Vulcans, a logical and stoic race of people who live somewhere in the universe. The greeting of the Vulcans is a raised hand in which the fingers are split to form a V and the saying "live long and prosper." This greeting is taken from the Jewish faith. The actor Leonard Nemo, the first Vulcan (Spock), was a Jew and attended synagogue as a child. At the end of the Jewish service, the priest pronounced Aaron's blessings, found in Numbers 6:22-27. The last word of the blessing is "shalom," and the custom is for the priest to raise his hand and form the Hebrew letter for the "S" in shalom (which looks like a weird W). This is the Hebrew letter "*shin*." The Rabbi's priestly blessing and hand gesture remarkably resemble the Vulcan hand gesture for long life and prosperity. Obviously, Leonard Nemo drew from his childhood when he acted out the Vulcan's greeting.

Shalom is a multifaceted concept. The word is translated as "peace," but the idea is much more than peace. Nemo understood that his Vulcan greeting of a long and prosperous life reflected the more expansive idea of shalom.

Shalom conveys the idea of completeness, soundness, health, contentment, prosperity, and welfare. As Benjamin Corey (2016, 38–63) explains, shalom means everything being as God intended it to be. Creation, before sin, was a place of shalom. Relationships were pure. God fellowshipped with man and woman. All of creation was friends with Adam and Eve. All was good. There were three important aspects related to this perfect world. First, honor and kindness were pervasive. Second, there was perfect fellowship, and third, personal health and wellbeing were normal. God gave Adam and Eve goals to care for the earth and to increase their community. Shalom was not to be contained; it was to be shared. Yet when sin came, the perfect world was lost. Later in human history, Jesus came to restore what had been lost.

What makes us captive? It is the will (the desire) to sin, which leads to the opposite of shalom. One quickly sees in the Fall that Adam and Eve lost all relational connection. Each was concerned about their own wellbeing, not that of the other. In place of honoring each other, they accused each other. Sin broke relationships, and it destroyed health and wellbeing. By the end of Genesis, sin is in full bloom. Conflict and broken relationships reach all levels of society. The end of Genesis shows that even families were murderous, fractured, and broken. Because of selfishness, God's goals of unity, honoring each other, caring for the earth, and expanding a peaceful world were turned to exploitation, murder, and war.

The addiction to sin leads to a world that God never intended. God responds to sin by showing mercy and giving grace. God loves creation. God acts by bringing the nature of the Trinity to a broken world. Through the Trinity, God demonstrates sacrificial love. God's objective is to use love to restore shalom. And by God's grace gifted through faith, the nature of God is planted in the believer's heart. We become loving by being virtuous. We can dance.

Rainbow World was created in the Garden of Eden. Everyone loved dancing, they danced, and they honored and praised each other. The Garden of Eden was selfless. Then sin came, and selfishness became the new human nature. Sin produced selfish human behaviors, and the dancing stopped. God, through God's Son, Jesus Christ, approached humanity with a solution. Through faith in Christ, God would gift humans God's grace. They could start rebuilding Rainbow World. By grace they could again dance. By grace they could practice virtues that lead to shalom and once again experience acceptance.

Human/Divine Drama and Revelation

God established Rainbow World. Its foundation is a loving community of selflessness for each other. The dance of Rainbow World is the dance of selfless love. If you want to teach people to dance, the best way is to show them the dance. As we have seen in the Trinity, God demonstrates love, honor, sacrifice, and praise for the Other. This is the dance. The dance produces oneness, harmony, and unity. Jesus, the revealed Word of God, and the Holy Spirit teach us how they dance.

Adam Dodds (2017, 24), a writer and pastor from New Zealand, explains that Jesus did not leave behind an infallible written code or even rules on the correct way to administer the sacraments. What Jesus left behind was a fellowship. God is dramatic and involved in the history of humanity. God is a fellowship of the Father, Son, and Holy Spirit, interacting with humankind in the drama of life. We know God is dramatic because of the numerous stories we see in scripture of God's mighty acts. In addition, we also hear testimonies of the followers of God that attest to God's mighty acts in their lives. God interacts, and God's relational interaction is a drama. Through the relational drama, there is revelation. The drama reveals truth. The Bible is a history of revelations produced by relational interactions (Ott, Strauss, and Tennent 2010, 315). God, through trinitarian relatedness, fully communicates God's self (Rahner 1997, 101–2). As we learn the stories of God's interaction with humanity, we learn who God is and who we are.

Jesus's teachings and sermons are not a PowerPoint presentation on the complexities of Leviticus or Deuteronomy. They are not workshops on theology or conferences about the dogmas of faith. Jesus makes no presentations on the right amount of water to use in baptism, the correct age to baptize, or even how often one should be baptized. Nor are there details on Communion. Does it have to be wine and unleavened bread? Should we invite everyone to come to the Table, or should those receiving the elements first be administered a theological exam? As much as we would all like a detailed conference by Jesus on the sacraments, what we actually have are stories.

What Jesus's teachings and life are about is human drama. The drama of being at a wedding and turning water to wine and a mother's confusion (John 2:1-11). The human drama of the prodigal son and all the human interaction that took place around the wayward son (Luke 15:11-32). The drama about the Samaritan woman at the well, her life, story, and the disciples' confusion (John 4:4-42). The drama of the ten healed lepers and the issue of showing gratitude (Luke 17:12-19). The blind man by the pool that was able to see and all the human interactions that followed (John 9). The parable about the Good Samaritan and all the human drama of the different actors in that story (Luke 10:25-37). The death of Lazarus (John 11), the busyness of Martha (Luke 10:38-42), the tax collector and the Pharisee in the temple (Luke 18:9-14), the acceptance of the prostitute (Luke 7:36-50), the rejection of the Pharisees (Matthew 23). The Gospels contain so much drama. The gospel message is revealed through human interactions. Through the community, its relational interactions, we understand God's Kingdom.

There is a reason for this: the dance is a dance of relationships. Most everything Jesus teaches and does points to relatedness—that is, how to love others. The dance is selfless love and what that should look like. The lessons on dancing are stories about life, relationships, and love, which leads the disciple to greater self-awareness. Jesus invites us to join the dance of the Trinity. Come dance with us, and dance as we dance.

For the sake of illustration, think of it this way. Let us say that your daughter goes to high school each day, and there are hundreds of students in the school. But one day, she comes home and announces she has a boyfriend. She is in love. Because of her love, this young man becomes known to your family. The announcement is followed by her dreamy description of how amazing he is. He is glorified and praised by your daughter, thus separating him from the hundreds of other people in the school. Love reveals. Only because of God's love, expressed in the Trinity, do we know the Father, Son, and Holy Spirit. They glorify and praise each other, and as a consequence, they are known. To love someone and then to want to reveal them to others is just part of the experience of love. What grandparent is not ready to quickly reveal a picture of their beloved grandchild? Rainbow World is about revealing each other through praise and honor and not glorifying ourselves.

Jesus does a type of PowerPoint message in the Gospel of Matthew (5 and 6)—one of the few. In this conference, the Sermon on the Mount, Jesus talks about human relatedness in the Kingdom of God. He mentions Levitical law from the Old Testament, primarily explaining that people misunderstood the law. Instead of diminishing the law, Jesus says the law is more demanding than they think. The law says to not murder; Jesus says hate is murder. The law says not to commit adultery; Jesus says lust is adultery. The law says an eye for an eye; Jesus says when ordered to walk a mile, walk the second mile, and give your shirt when your coat is taken. Jesus says to forgive debtors, turn the other cheek, mean what you say without swearing an oath, and not be in conflict with others while making offerings to God.

God is pulling humanity into the fellowship of the Trinity. The gospel message is a story about reconciliation with God and each other. The stories tell us what love looks like, moving love from an abstract concept to real life. Love involves virtues; otherwise, love is so abstract that it is meaningless. In the Sermon on the Mount, Jesus moves the conversation from the Law to a deeper level that explains the intent of the Law. And the dramas that Jesus lives and the stories he tells illustrate the real meaning of the Law. God's goal is to empower us to live in such a radical way that we have peace by showing honor and glory to our Creator and to each other. The purpose of the virtuous life is to experience shalom—that is, communion. Grace is the key: it motivates us to act virtuously.

Marriage, Modeling God's Oneness

Marriage is an example of the dance, a prototype of oneness, intimacy, and community. In Mark 10, Jesus talks about marriage. He says that God made males and females at creation, and each will leave their parents, and through marriage, the two shall become one. Marriage is an expression of oneness. As spouses soon realize, one gives up what they want in marriage, so the other has what they want. Jesus made it simple to understand when he said, "You should love your neighbor as yourself" (Matthew 22:39). Marriage is putting ourselves in the place of our spouse. We are trying to see their needs as they see those needs. And once we understand them, we try to meet those needs. Our marriage becomes a book of love stories about what selfless love looks like day in and day out.

The Christian vows of marriage illustrate the selfless ideals of marriage. The vows ask each to be committed in sickness and in health, in want and in plenty, in sorrow and in joy. Married couples, soon into their marriages, can tell stories of love in the context of sickness, want, and sorrow. What is it like to be loved and cared for when sick, when in need, when sorrowful? A successful marriage is a drama of living virtuously, making decisions that put the other person first. Our prayer is that grace will inspire us to love as we would want to be loved.

A successful marriage allows for the unique personhood of each, and marriage asks each to honor the other above oneself. Spouses are cheerleaders for each other, not for themselves. Love results in public honor of the other person. The praise and honor of each other—selfless love—is the basis of oneness. Oneness is not control of the other or sameness. Oneness is the freedom to be unique while glorifying the other. Glorification allows each person to be known as uniquely special. We become, as seen in the Trinity, messengers of the greatness of those we love. The virtuous life is a life that loves in tangible ways. Our virtues are seen by how we glorify the "other."

Grace Reveals God's Nature

The Catholic theologian Karl Rahner (1961, I:310) explains that grace is God's form of communication. God wants to communicate who God is. God is love. In fact, all of creation and all of human history is to convey the fact that God is love. Grace is God giving God's nature to humanity. The passion to live in a relationship with God and others is God's grace, and it reveals God's nature. Therefore, in the believer's life, grace inspires us to live a virtuous life, which communicates God's nature to humanity.

Jesus explained that to know him was to know the Father. This revelation was one reason for Jesus's crucifixion; he claimed to be equal to God (John 5:18). The Jewish leaders were infuriated by Jesus's claim. They stated that Jewish law demanded that Jesus die as a blasphemer (John 19:7). However, Jesus was who he said he was. Jesus was equal to God. Paul explains that Jesus, being fully equal to God, humbled himself and became a man in order to glorify his Father. God raised Jesus from the dead and exalted his son above all others (Philippians 2:6-11). The Father glorified his Son. The glorification of the "Other" showed the nature of God. The love between the Father and Son—their praise, honor, and sacrifice for each other—showed us how to dance.

This idea of love is demonstrated by honor and glorification, revealing the uniqueness of the ones we love. The amazing thing about the dance of selfless love is that it does not produce conformity. It produces distinction and uniqueness because we show love by pointing out how the person we love is exceptional. The dance also reveals that we are amazing. But that announcement is made by others. We each become known as exceptional persons because those who love us reveal who we are.

The theologian Rahner (1961, I:310) explains that God has but one plan, and that is to pour forth "the love which he himself is." Augustine connected grace to love. Grace changes selfish greed (concupiscence) to selfless love (charity). God changes Christians by giving them a love for "the good" and love for others. Grace frees Christians from seeing others as a means to self-satisfaction (Haight 1979, 49). As Rahner (1961, I:311) explains, humankind is created so that God can bestow God's love into human hearts. Humans are to be a light, a testimony of God's love. God shows them mercy and gives them grace, and his followers show each other love by God's grace. Through the passion from grace, the Christian is free to relate to others in selfless ways. Augustine cites Romans 12:21: "Do not be overcome by evil, but overcome evil with good." Augustine (2010, 12) interprets this verse to mean that grace pulls us away from selfishness and to selflessness. Grace is the passion to love, and love is the act and attitude of honor and praise for another above oneself.

The motivation to dance comes from grace, and it reveals God's nature. God demonstrates the dance by how the Father, Son, and Holy Spirit love and are loved by each other. God gifts us God's grace, the same passion God has that produces the virtuous life of love. The Godhead presents and explains the dance through scripture, which are stories of life. We see the dance through the testimony of God's love for Adam and Eve, Noah, Abraham, Moses, Israel, and in the life of Christ. God interacting with humankind is a drama that reveals the dance. Jesus explained, before his departure, that he would leave behind a dance instructor, who would be the Holy Spirit. The source of the wind that changes us is God's Spirit (John 14:15-17, 25-26).

The Dance of Honor

Karl Barth, a Swiss theologian, helps us understand the dance. Barth stated, "The God who comes to the church is the God who loves in freedom by giving himself unconditionally in love" (Barth and Johnson 2019, 173). Jesus freely forgave repentant sinners and honored them. Jesus decided to love humanity by selflessly accepting humanities' sins on the cross and glorifying those who seek forgiveness for their sins (Luke 22:42). Jesus put it this way while praying to his Father: "The glory that you have given me I have given to them, that they may be one even as we are one" (John 17:22). Jesus transferred the honor and glory the Father gave him to his disciples.

In the book, *Relational Missions*, honor and glory are explained from both theological and sociological perspectives. God's creation was based on glorification, and the relationship between God and humanity was one of sharing honor (Thomas 2020, 60–67). The following explains the gospel message from the perspective of honor and shame.

"Back to God's Village," a short cartoon video found on
YouTube and other websites, explains the gospel message
from the honor and shame perspective. It illustrates what
the gospel looks like when presented as an honor and
shame story. The video explains that God created man and
woman and gave them great honor. God walked with
them and allowed them to enjoy God's creation. Even
while they were naked, they had no shame. However, by
seeking more honor and glory for themselves, they sinned.
As a result, they were ashamed. Because God is honorable
and man and woman are not, God sent them away from
God's garden. Their shame caused rejection. They lost
their honor; they no longer belonged. All of their
descendants lived in the same inherited family shame, like
being children of a murderer or prostitute. In an effort to
recover honor, humankind separated themselves into
groups and tried to say their group was more honorable
than others. They often fought each other, trying to gain
the respect of the other groups and be honored and
glorified by others. God sent God's Son, Jesus, the only
honorable person on earth. Jesus said he would take our
shame if we would honor him. (Thomas 2020, 61)

God's creation was initially a place of glorification and
fellowship. God, Adam, and Eve delighted in each other as they
shared the experience of Earth. They glorified each other. Sin
destroyed the fellowship, and the human community was
fractured on all levels. Humans, to recover their honor, became
selfish and demanded recognition from each other. Speaking
about oppressors of Israel, the prophet Habakkuk said, "They
[oppressors] are dreaded and fearsome; their justice and dignity
[honor] go forth from themselves" (Habakkuk 1:7). The
oppressors force others to glorify them. As the "Back to God's

Village" video explains, humankind developed groups so that their group could be honored by other groups. This approach resulted in racism, prejudice, injustice, ethnocentrism, mobs, conflicts, and wars. Because of sin, we have lost our glory, and now we form groups and demand others honor us.

God sent His son to restore community and peace through the cross. Jesus gave up his honor by his sacrifice on the cross. Through the cross, he honored God and humanity. Jesus's surrender to the cross was an act that showed honor for the other and not for himself. He honored his Father by being obedient to his Father. God wanted to present a way of reconciliation to the world and restore community. In order to offer reconciliation, Jesus honored humanity by taking their shame of sin. The cross was a statement by Jesus of honor for God and for us. Jesus said, "If I glorify myself, my glory is nothing. It is my Father who glorifies me, of whom you say, 'He is our God.'" (John 8:54). We can conclude that the cross is about selfless love and the glorification of others.

The dance is an interchange of honor, where one never claims honor for him or herself. Jesus provides a way for the repentant to regain God's honor. God's acceptance comes through us honoring God's Son. As any parent knows, the best way to gain a parent's love is to love their children. As Jesus explained in John 12:26, "If anyone serves me, the Father will honor him." The dance of love is one of honor and praise. This is the dance God seeks to restore. We honor others, not ourselves. Selflessness is expressed in many different ways: serving, giving, hospitality, kindness, sacrificing, mourning, humility, humor, surrendering, and obedience, to name just a few ways to express honor to God and others. To understand the dance, one must simply read the stories of God's interactions with humanity found in the Bible. In them we see God's true nature—the one grace is bringing to our lives. Those stories show us the divine dance of honor and glorification of the Other.

Communion

The Eucharist is the classical term used to refer to the Last Supper that Jesus shared with his disciples before his crucifixion. (*Eucharistia* is Greek for thanksgiving.) The Last Supper is often called the Lord's Supper. The term *Lord's Supper* was used in the first century and draws upon the verses in 1 Corinthians 11 about the Lord's Supper. Later in church history, the Protestant churches refuted the power of the Eucharist to save and began to use the term "Communion."

Communion captures the idea of a community around the table in fellowship. The central focus of that community is the person of Jesus Christ. Jesus, as the focus, brings the diverse community into communion. The unity of the community and their diversity reflect God's power, which can reconcile people so that they can form fellowships that transcend ethnic, cultural, socio-economic, age, and gender differences.

The Lord's Supper was instituted to visualize, illustrate, and demonstrate love. It is the dance class's promotional video. Baptism is related to one's profession of faith in Christ. The Lord's Supper is related to selfless love for others and sharing our lives. In 1 Corinthians 11:17-34, Paul clearly presents the Lord's Supper in the context of relational reconciliation. After Paul explains the elements, Paul gives the criteria for receiving the Lord's Supper: "Let a person examine himself" before eating or drinking the Lord's Supper (1 Corinthians 11:28). Paul challenges the Corinthians to leave the table, heal broken relationships, and return and take the bread and wine. He adds that all are to be patient with each other and not be judgmental. This fellowship is more than doctrinal agreement; it is unity founded on getting along with each other (Cavanaugh 1998, 247).

As David Bosch (2011, 167–68), a professor of missions, explains, the Lord's Supper is not a meal of mutual tolerance. Rather, the Lord's Supper announces a new body in which those at the table are being transformed. The fellowship of the Table is one in which we share our lives with each other. Implied in this shared life is a willingness to share each other's burdens, to invest in other's lives, to serve, to care, to be generous, and to be a friend. Once at the table, all are reminded of the importance of selfless love. The bread in hand reminds us of Christ's sacrifice, the life given to honor others. And the cup reminds us of the new covenant of grace. God's grace is given so that we can practice a virtuous life—a selfless life that develops communion away from the table.

Forgiveness

If we lived in a perfect world, one where there was no selfishness, there would be no need for forgiveness. Forgiveness is acceptance after an offense. In Matthew 6:14, Jesus explained that when people sin against you, forgive them as God forgave you. This scripture illustrates that forgiveness focuses on those who have hurt us. To forgive, we first must identify people that have disappointed or offended us. Part of the Rainbow World dance is accepting those who sinned against us. Later, in Mathew 18:21-22, Jesus explained that forgiveness was a way of life. He told Peter there was no number of times one was limited to forgive. Furthermore, Jesus (Mark 11:25) and Paul (1 Corinthians 11:17-34) explained that prayer was to be a time of reflection and forgiveness. We recall those who offended us, and we accept them. We show mercy and do not give them what they deserve, which would be retaliation.

Grace produces a passion for forgiving. Augustine refers to Stephen as he was being stoned in Acts 7:54-60. He forgave his killers as they killed him. Augustine adds that "hate" keeps one from forgiving. The offended elevates the offense to the point that it is the focus of the entire relationship. Augustine advocates prayer for grace to forgive. Grace gives the offended the desire to accept the offender. An important facet of the dance of Rainbow World is the grace to forgive those who offend us. Augustine (2007, 94) repeatedly reminds his readers of the Lord's Prayer: "Forgive us our debts as we forgive our debtors". God dances the dance God expects us to dance. Later, in Chapter 6, we will look at what happens to grace when we do not forgive and allow bitterness to rule.

⌘

How do Christians justify good deeds? The challenge before the Christian is to live a selfless life, a virtuous life. Virtues and disciplines are the foundation of selflessness. Virtues are the visible ways we love others. Peter reminds us of God's Word: "Be holy, for I am holy" (1 Peter 1:6). How can we live holy lives? In the next chapter, we will look at good deeds. Protestants struggle with the idea of good works. The saying often heard is that "we are saved by faith and not works." This saying tends to diminish good works and complicate the question of doing good deeds.

4. Doing Good: Dancing Is What Makes Us Dancers

Humans obey what gives them pleasure.

The Presbyterian revivalist preacher James McGready, of the early 1800s, is credited with being one of the sparks of the Second Great Awakening on the American frontier. This revival movement swept through Kentucky, Tennessee, and other surrounding USA territories and states over many years. It involved large outdoor crusades that lasted days, consisting of hundreds and even thousands of participants and new converts to Christianity. In part, the Christianization of America and its outreach to the world through missions has its origin in the Second Great Awakening. The denomination I am affiliated with, the Cumberland Presbyterian Church, was born from the Second Great Awakening. The Methodists were also huge beneficiaries of this Great Awakening, as well as other denominations. Some of his sermons survived and have been printed. One of them talks about grace and represents the theology of Reformed and evangelical/revivalist Christianity. His revivalistic approach, which stressed conversion and the expectation of transformation, is seen in his sermon on grace. Within a collection of McGrady's sermons, there is a sermon about grace. The sermon is titled "The Superabounding Grace of God" (Smith 1837, 197–212).

Grace is More Than a Future Hope

One of the remarkable things about McGready's sermon is his emphasis on the hopelessness of sin. Sin is understood as an enslaving illness or poison. No doubt his emphasis on the enslavement of sin resonated with those that heard his sermon.

Everyone could identify with feeling imprisoned by their sins. McGready referred to the human condition as "the venomous and infectious nature of sin" that poisons everything (Smith 1837, 200). As a consequence of this infection, the heart hates God, and humankind is controlled by sin. Humans are blinded and trapped by sin (Smith 1837, 204).

McGready speaks of grace as the solution to sin. However, if you look closely, it appears that he is talking about salvation and not the specific force of grace. McGready says that grace—that is salvation—makes us aware of our sins and dissatisfied with how we live our lives.

> Almighty grace can subdue millions of sins, and
> deliver all true believers completely from them,
> for it restores the spiritually dead to life, it
> sanctifies all their powers and faculties, and, in
> due time, will bring them to greater abundance
> of glory and bliss than Adam lost, and will
> confirm them in the full enjoyment of heaven
> through the boundless ages of eternity, which
> clearly proves that where sin abounded grace
> did much more abound. (Smith 1837, 203)

Grace is presented as the way to confront sin by subduing "millions of sins" and delivering "all believers completely from them." McGready continues, stating that "in due time" grace has its full effect. His point is that once we die, we find righteousness. There is no rationale given as to how we are to live changed lives as Christians. Faith is the focus; good works are secondary to faith. The Christian hope of holiness is found in heaven. All that said, McGready still believes Christians should live holy (transformed) lives somehow.

The saved, says McGready, discover "that their hearts are totally depraved and opposed to the holy nature of the law," unlike the non-Christians, who are "the thoughtless and guilty multitude" all around us (Smith 1837, 206). The idea is that salvation brings awareness of sin. Good works are tricky. We want to stop sinning and do good, but good works are more about remorse than delight. As McGready explained, "Shortly your beloved Jesus will send for you and take you home to your father's house, where sin and all its bitter effects are banished" (Smith 1837, 206).

McGready, like most other revivalist Reformed preachers, explained that the key was faith, not works. He clarified that God expects Christians not to be hypocrites. God only accepts their good works if those works come from their faith. "Have you been brought to see that your own righteousness, your prayers, tears, groans, vows, and good works, are but as dross and dung in the sight of the Holy God" (Smith 1837, 210). Without faith our efforts to act righteously are wasted energy. Thus, by faith and deeds, explains McGready, we can be confident of our salvation (Smith 1837, 210).

McGready demonstrates the struggle Protestants have with good works. Faith is central to salvation, and it secures our future in heaven. We should feel bad about our sins. Feeling bad about our sins is really the main point. But our hope is in our faith and our eternal reward. Faith on earth is our way to future righteousness in heaven. As McGready explains, even non-believers can do good works. Thus, faith is the key and good works are, well, a little problematic.

I contend that McGready's view only gives a partial understanding of how grace changes us. It does make us feel discontent with our sinful nature, but grace does much more. Grace is not a sensation of misery. And salvation and the gift of grace are not just a hope for change after our death. Many Christians leaders rightfully react to revivalist theology that only talks about feeling miserable about our sins. Evangelism can be seen as judgmental and negative and not hopeful.

Obeying What Gives Us Pleasure

One of the most ardent students of Augustine, Cornelius Jansen of Finland, became a professor and priest in Scandinavia. As a theology professor in the early 1600s, Jansen dedicated himself to an intense study of Augustine. He wrote a bulky book on Augustine called *Augustinus*. Before it was published, he died. His disciples published it in 1640. Jansen puts a more positive spin on salvation than the revivalist preacher McGready. Jansen's book created an uproar in the Roman Catholic Church. The Roman Catholic Church—in particular, the Jesuit Order—believed that the ideas in the book, which produced a group of devotees, were supportive of Luther and other Protestants (Minor 2016, 141–42). In fact, Jansen disavowed the Protestants when alive, but he expressed appreciation for their enthusiasm. He hoped that the Roman Catholic Church could capture that enthusiasm. There were many meetings by influential Church leaders, and the end result was that Jansenism[2] was ruled heretical by the Roman Catholic Church.

Jansen does a great job of explaining Augustinian grace as a force of passion. Jansen explained that humans obey what gives them pleasure—that is, what they desire. The natural man is forced to obey or follow their natural desires (Segundo 1973,

---

[2] Jansenism was a movement within the Roman Catholic Church that used Jansen's book *Augustinus* as its guide. The Jesuits feared that the followers of Jansenism were part of the Protestant Reformation, and the Jesuits were the ones that actually named them "Jansenists". Jansenism moved away from their founder's focus on Augustine and begin to adopt ideas that were unacceptable to the Catholic Church. The movement was rejected by the Church and ruled heretical.

2:20). As Paul cynically explained, "their god is their belly," and they delight in what they should be ashamed of (Philippians 3:19). Natural pleasures enslave the sinner. McGready's sermon did a great job pointing this out. No doubt, the hearers felt trapped by their human nature. Therefore, man is not free. Jansen's idea was, "Grace comes to endow good with the delight it lacks" (Segundo 1973, 2:20).

The disciples of Jansen, after his death, were inspired by his writings because they offered a way for people to be excited about changing. Jansen's disciples wanted to reform the Catholic Church, to bring piety back to their Church. The Jansenists were concerned about the moral laxity of the Church (Minor 2016, 141, 143), and Augustine's ideas on grace were the ticket to holiness.

Grace breaks the back of sin when it makes doing good more pleasurable than doing evil. There is a war going on in all believers, and their natural passions war against the grace-inspired passions. McGready believed that the war went poorly, and at best, victory on this earth resembled disgust over our sins. The Christian was to be miserable about their sins and attempt to be disciplined. The motivation to be good, to change, was based on the embarrassment of being bad. McGready preached to surrender to God, renounce your sins, and try to live a holy life. Jansen explained that living a holy life could be more than feeling misery and trying hard. Not surprisingly, McGready and other revivalists were accused of being...yes, Pelagianists. McGready, reflecting the thought of other Protestants, understood how grace helped one feel bad about sin, but it was not totally clear how it produced the virtuous life.

The Roman Church had meetings and debates for decades over Jansen's ideas. His ideas made it all the way to the Pope's audience, where most of the ideas were condemned (O'Callaghan 2016, 208). One issue was about free will. Jansen's idea of following one's delight was controversial for the Catholics because it sounded like enslavement. The church feared that grace could swallow up free will; thus, one is enslaved by grace. For this reason, and other reasons, the church rejected Jansen's idea of grace (Segundo 1973, 2:20). Ironically, the Roman Catholic Church concluded that being delighted in doing godly things was slavery. As the liberation theologian and Jesuit priest Juan Luis Segundo (1973, 2:20) explains, grace and freedom are not in conflict. In fact, they can be combined. In reality, Jansen had explained how good works could be done and not be a hardship. And because doing good things was pleasurable, the godly lived in freedom, doing righteousness.

Jansen made grace sound more hopeful than McGready. Salvation takes the sinner past disgust over their sin to joy in righteousness. For Jansen grace was a force within that allowed one to be delighted in doing good works that pleased God. Jansen's grace is like being overweight and having a drug that makes healthy, low-calorie food taste fantastic. Grace changed the sinner, said Jansen, by changing their delights. Grace allowed one to live a joyful and changed life while on this earth.

To put this another way, those in Rainbow World dance because it is pleasing to dance. It is their delight to dance. God expects His followers to dance, and because of God's grace, they enjoy dancing. This arrangement is a win-win: believers meet God's behavioral expectations, and at the same time, believers live in freedom. McGready correctly observed that sinners find no delight in their sin. Everyone wants to escape loneliness, and they want to dance and to belong. Jansen correctly observed that the believer finds pleasure in righteousness. Believers find pleasure in what makes them belong. Grace combines pleasure, freedom and righteousness.

The Problem with Grace as Identity

Professor Roger Haight (1979, 73) notes that grace, under the influence of Aquinas, moved from a healing force to a state of being. The next logical step is to separate grace from righteous acts and attribute grace to simply being declared righteous. Being proclaimed accepted by God is the legendary idea that every player in the tournament gets a winner's trophy after the soccer tournament. This is what some Protestants did: grace became a gift, and that gift was a new identity. The new "identity" gift was something they did not deserve.

Augustine said faith is where one gets the energy to act; we become what we gladly do. In fact, this was what Aquinas was after: our identity and our acts are inseparable. At some point in theological history, the two were separated, and that is when the confusion started.

As time passed in the church, many leaders diminished grace as a force to act righteously and explained that grace was God accepting the undeserving. The focus was on grace as a gift of identity. As a result, a person was proclaimed righteous regardless of his or her works. We are all winners, and we all get a trophy. It is only natural that the idea of universalism became the next logical step for some theologians. If God is love and grace is acceptance, wouldn't an all-loving God accept everyone, regardless of their deeds or religious beliefs? Universalism is the idea that God loves and accepts everyone. All are chosen by God regardless of religion or their lack of religion. Universalism is hyper-election. God in God's infinite love accepts everyone. Universalism sees grace as infinite love, and God accepts all the undeserving regardless.

Most Protestants and Catholic theologians are not universalists. But Luther did minimize works when he explained,

"Works, since they are irrational things, cannot glorify God, although they may be done to the glory of God, if faith be present" (Luther 1520, 22). The idea is to minimize dancing and maximize identity as a dancer. The Christian's identity comes from faith, and to a lesser extent, from what one does. The minimizing of works later led some theologians to question if works had any value at all.

In Luther's Rainbow World everyone is a horrible dancer, and they know they are. Luther's solution was that Christians should be disgusted about their sins. "You cannot dance! And you should feel horrible." You are a dancer who dances very poorly, but all people that are proclaimed to be dancers go to heaven. In Luther's Rainbow World, when you get to heaven, you will then dance perfectly.

Let me share three ways to justify good works when emphasizing faith and not works. And in each case, I will point out the problem.

One approach comes from remorse. We have remorse over our sins and feel bad. The revivalist preachers did a great job of pointing out how hopeless Christians are. Christians distance themselves from sinful behavior because they feel remorse over their sins. The feeling of shame produces abstinence from sin. It is like being overweight and confronted with a table of desserts. Our disgust about our weight stops us from eating. This is certainly not a joyful way to live one's faith—shaming oneself to do godly things and not to do sinful things is exhausting. Besides, eventually one tries to find a way to escape their shame, even if it involves denial.

Another approach is to do good works out of gratitude. God accepts us and gives us a new identity, and we should be grateful. The way to express gratitude to God is to act in ways that please God. Gratitude is then an exchange in trade. Our good works are repayment for God's acceptance. However, gratitude should be an expression of humility that acknowledges dependence on others. It is not payment for the gift received. If we are given a gift, are we obligated to return a gift? If our good works are repayment for our gift, then we are working.

The third approach some advocate is to see atonement as Jesus Christ hiding us from God's view. The idea is that when the poor dancer is paired with a great dancer, the judge only sees the great dancer. We claim Christ's righteousness. God only sees the fantastic dancer, Jesus. By faith in Christ, one now transfers their obligation for good works to Christ. We are hidden. Atonement then means that Jesus hides us from the judge's view. Our confidence is in Jesus, and our works are not that important.

However, Augustine (2014, ch. 16) explains that atonement frees us from human carnal desires (concupiscence) and regenerates us with the Spirit of grace. The Bible does not teach atonement as Christ hiding our sins. We do not use Christ to hide from the judge. Atonement is the idea of being infused with power. We are covered with grace. By atonement through Christ, we experience joy in God (Augustine 2014, ch. 16). Grace is not a cover that hides us; it is a force which flows in the believer, replacing selfishness with selflessness. Our nature is reborn to be like God's nature.

Love involves good works. We need tangible ways to love others if we want to form a community. Using dancing as a metaphor for love, we can say that by dancing we create a community of mutual acceptance, and we belong. When we dance, we form a loving community. Christ comes into our hearts, and by grace we are transformed. Atonement is God's Spirit empowering us to love, to do good works, resulting in making us likable.

Luther minimized good works and focused on faith. Faith, he believed, gave us status in God's eyes. His perspective was that we were priests, kings, free people, children of God, and co-heirs as believers in Christ. Faith gave the believer this type of identity. These positions of status were not literal societal positions a person had in their community. They were positions a person held in the divine realm because they were in Christ. Luther separated Aquinas's inseparable relationship between performance and identity. The impact was to emphasize identity over performance. Consequently, many Protestant theologians then scrambled trying to justify why good behavior should be part of the Christian's life. These leaders believed in living holy and righteous lives; some were even Pietist. But without grace, all their explanations tended to fall short. At times they sounded like Pelagianists. Without the idea of a power from within that makes us willing and able to please God, works become, well, works.

Roger Haight (1979, 156), a Catholic, notes that Luther probably experienced the type of grace that Aquinas explained. Luther had an experience that elevated and changed him. He was flooded with passion and energy to do things for God and others that he had never done before. Luther did good works. He was divinized, and he was an enthusiastic and free participant in God's mission. Luther experienced grace, but he did not realize that all his works were evidence that he was an enthusiastic and free participant in God's mission. Faith and works did not need to be separated. Augustinian grace showed the way. This understanding was Aquinas's point about grace. Grace and identity go together, and consequently, so do works and faith. As Paul explained, "But by the grace of God I am what I am, and his grace toward me was not in vain. On the contrary, I worked harder than any of them, though it was not I, but the grace of God that is with me" (I

Corinthians 15:10). Paul said, I danced, and I danced pretty well; but it was not me. God in me made me a good dancer.

John Calvin, on the other hand, was more inclined toward Augustinian grace. Calvin said, "Guilt is from nature, whereas sanctification is from supernatural grace" (Calvin 1509, bk. 2, ch. 2, sec. 7). Calvin speaks of the transformation of the soul by grace, thus leaning toward grace as a force. The natural appetite is suppressed, and the mind is renewed. He agreed with Luther that all of the human heart is corrupt, but grace replaces corrupt desires with godly desires. With grace, a person is free. Grace, works and freedom, say both Calvin and Augustine, are integrated. Doing good from a passion for doing good is living in freedom. Consistent with Augustine, Calvin (1509, bk. 2, ch. 2, secs. 4–9) explained that humans were not free when they were jailed by wills that lusted to sin.[3]

Why People Do Good Deeds

There is another reality, one that is obvious to many. Lots of non-believers dance, and some dance very well. This observation was Pelagius's main argument for promoting that one's own will and self-discipline could produce a holy life and salvation. Why do non-believers dance? Below are different assumptions about non-believers doing good deeds.

---

[3] In 1542 John Calvin established a clergy-governed theocracy in the city of Geneva. By all accounts it was a disaster. Cavin forced compliance to religious practices, such as the Lord's Supper, church attendance, and moral codes of conduct. If a citizen did not comply, they were punished—in some cases, tortured and executed. Despite Cavin's appreciation and promotion of grace as how to motivate righteousness, he reverted to the customs of his day. He used civil power to force religious control. Even Augustine believed the state (Rome) and church, working together, could Christianize the world. I doubt Augustine would have ever gone as far as what Calvin did in Geneva.

1. **Human Dancers:** God made humans in God's image with certain innate abilities to do good. All humans can dance. Their dance is the shadow of God that is still in them after Adam and Eve's fall from grace (Genesis 3, the Garden, the first Rainbow World). The Chinese writer Watchman Nee referred to this as the "latent power of the soul" (Nee 1972). Nee explained that the dance is false: it appears to be godly, but in reality, it has self-serving motives. The dance is driven by human nature (Nee 1972, 20). This view is what McGready also said: people do good things for the wrong reasons. Their dance is not authentic. The Italian theology professor Paul O'Callaghan (2016, 206) agrees when he says their dance is "camouflaged vices." Thus, the reason or motive for doing good is more important than the good deeds. Godliness is dancing for the right reasons, and those reasons revolve around faith in Christ. Non-Christians do good works from the afterglow of creation, and they are in vain. Those works do not matter without faith in Christ.

2. **Deceived Dancers:** Another common idea is that both Christians and non-believers are horrible dancers. The difference is that Christians know they are terrible dancers. The non-Christians do not admit they are terrible dancers. Christians believe their dancing is not very good and non-Christians believe their dancing is great. They say things like, "I am not a murderer or a bad person." As Luther explained, by faith in Christ, we acknowledge that we are not good dancers (we are sinners) and that God has forgiven and accepted us as we are (Haight 1979, 90). Christians are poor dancers, and they know it. Non-Christians are poor dancers, but they will not admit it. The non-Christians have deceived themselves into believing

the dancing they do is better than it is. They are righteous in their own eyes and expect God to appreciate what good dancers they are (Proverbs 21:2).

3. **Born Dancers:** In this view, everyone is a dancer, both Christians and non-Christians. We are all made in God's image, and we are all dancers. In fact, we were gifted this extraordinary gift at birth. Grace involves being born rich and not fully realizing how rich one is because he or she has always been rich. We were born dancers, and we dance, often unaware we are dancing. Humans are social beings; it is our godly nature. "Grace goes above and beyond the boundaries of the Church and in some way reaches humanity as a whole" (Segundo 1973, 2:103). Christians and non-Christians do good things, which is evidence that God's grace is universal. This concept is called universalism. "Christ came to save all human beings, not only every individual but all together" (Segundo 1973, 2:105). God has proclaimed all of humanity as accepted, and God's grace is so expansive and so deep that all have received it. Everyone, at some level, does good works. Coming to faith is realizing our identity—an identity we have whether we know it or not. God accepts both non-Christians and Christians. Everyone does good works well enough.

4. **Obligated Dancers:** The non-Christian may obtain a certain level of righteousness, but it is a righteousness that is based on obligation, self-discipline, fear of punishment, and/or legalism. The idea of the law is that it forces good works. The New Testament says the law falls short, but it does pressure sinners to live righteously (Romans 3:20). Communities, in the absence of grace, must establish boundaries and expectations for their members to follow.

Then those boundaries must be policed. The extreme fundamentalist religious groups are examples of this legalistic approach to good works. The members of the community conform to the group's expectations. People feel obligated to do good because of group pressure. No one wants to be punished or be an outcast. One of the consequences of forced conformity is that the moral and ethical standards will shift as society's laws and societal standards shift. Conformity is enforced by legalism and society's acceptance or rejection of behaviors. Goodness, as society defines it, is an obligation.

Augustine was trying to solve a problem. The problem is seen in the above explanations about doing good deeds. His innovation was about how to change and avoid the pitfalls seen above. Augustine explained how salvation resulted in good deeds. Those deeds were not based on human effort to behave, the self-deception that we are behaving better than we are, universal acceptance of all behaviors, or forced behaviors dictated by peer pressure. The discussion about grace was a discussion about what it means for a Christian to change and be different. Salvation, through faith and grace, offered a more realistic way to change than those above.

Salvation is a transition in direction, not a continuation in our current direction. Salvation is about change, not the glorification of an unchanged life. And salvation is about freedom in Christ, not Old Testament legalism. Christian salvation and transformation are a roar of energy from God in the heart of the repentant that makes good works a delight. That was Augustine's central point: grace makes change delightful. Grace makes believers relational by changing their actions and attitudes. The change cultivated by grace often does not conform to society's expectations. But grace infuses behaviors that are pleasing to God and build community.

The followers of Christ can experience freedom and pleasure in doing good. Their good deeds foster meaningful community. Grace brings freedom to the will and delight in doing good as God defines good.

The Problem with Grace as Acceptance

Another emphasis some have made with respect to grace is the idea that grace is acceptance. Some say that Rainbow World is not about dancing. Rather, it is about acceptance. Let us look at the idea of grace as acceptance. The logic is as follows: if God is love and all-powerful, God can undoubtedly love anyone. God's depth of love is seen in how God can accept the unacceptable and declare them righteous. Therefore, God's grace, understood as acceptance, shows how expansive God's love is when God accepts those no one else will accept. The gospel message becomes God accepts us. And evangelism emphasizes that we are to accept everyone as we have been accepted. The emphasis is not on behavior or works. What matters is acceptance.

In the context of grace as acceptance, the church's mission becomes a hypersensitivity to accepting others. If God accepts us, we must accept everyone. The point is not "change"; it is acknowledging our identity as a person whom God accepts, and then accepting everyone as they are. Accepting the poor, hungry, social outcasts, and marginalized is how we show grace to others. The sinners trapped in their sins are to be accepted. Evangelism becomes focused on helping the marginalized. Who has society rejected? Those are the ones whom we must accept as our demonstration of grace. We accept people unworthy of society's acceptance.

You ask, "Isn't accepting the marginalized part of the gospel's mandate?" It is. But the gospel mandate does not leave sinners or the marginalized in their misery. The church goes to the margins, but it does not stay there. We are to proclaim faith in Christ and announce the hope of transformative grace. Grace can change us. It can move us out of our misery. It can free us from the prison that selfishness puts us in. When Jesus discovered the prostitute in the street standing before a mob ready to stone her to death, he intervened. In so doing, he reached out to the marginalized. He stopped the mob. Then he turned to the prostitute and offered transformation: "Go, and from now on sin no more" (John 8:1-11). Grace can inspire us to sin no more. By grace and the virtues it inspires, we can act in ways that build community, acceptance, and belonging. Without grace, we accept unrepentant sinners and give them no hope of transformation and no hope of a loving community. How will the marginalized ever become part of our community if they cannot dance? By faith and grace, they can dance.

Grace changes us so that we behave in ways such that people can accept us. Why do we love God? Because God is virtuous and loving. God's actions toward humanity are sacrificial and selfless. Maybe it has never dawned on you, but because God is selfless, God is easy to like. That is what grace is doing in the believer; it is helping us to be virtuous and loving—in other words, to be acceptable. Bryant Myers, the former director of World Vision, a humanitarian relief agency, explains that the poor are not poor because they merely lack provision. True, the poor lack food, clothing and/or housing. But what they really lack, explains Myers, are the right relationships. Their poverty is the result of being outside of a healthy community (Winter et al. 2009, 607–9). To be whole, they need to be part of a healthy community. To be part of a healthy community, they too need to change and become healthy. Healthy churches and Christian groups do reach out to the marginalized, and they should. But ultimately, the marginalized have to make decisions that result in change. The "outcasts" are in a better position to change when a community is reaching out to them and sharing how faith, repentance and grace can make one virtuous and loving and part of a community.

Churches that preach acceptance of the marginalized and not transformation through grace find that the marginalized drain considerable time and resources and remain marginalized. Church leaders willingly give their time and resources as an expression of acceptance. But the unchanged person continues to live in misery. This produces the dance-less world where all stand around, wondering why there is no sense of belonging. Dancing is how we belong. If transformation is not part of the gospel message, through grace, then the marginalized continue to live in ways that have caused them to be rejected by society.

Where there is no expectation of transformation, the church becomes a self-centered community who feels good about accepting the marginalized. Oddly, the more broken the sinner is—the more dysfunctional they are—the better the church feels about accepting them. The church may feel great, but the sinner feels lost and disconnected. The behaviors that created isolation, poverty, and hardships continue. There is no dancing. The prostitute of John 8 would never find a community of belonging if she tried to join a church and continued in her prostitution. Prostitution destroys community. Jesus affirmed this when he said to sin no more. Faith brings grace and freedom along with change. If grace is not part of salvation, then the misery never stops, and community is never found.

The reality is that the virtuous life spelled out in the Bible is designed to build community. Without the deeds, without the dance, there is no loving community. How can we accept each other when we all behave so selfishly and poorly? First, we must renounce selfishness, and then we must change through grace-driven behaviors. Where there are no virtues, there is no dancing. Where there is no dancing, it is impossible to have a community.

Augustine's solution to sin was to dance! He believed that Christians were expected and empowered to live righteously. They could dance because salvation brought grace, which produced the desire and the ability to dance. By grace change and community were possible. As Segundo explains, Jesus said, "For I tell you, unless your righteousness exceeds that of the scribes and Pharisees, you will never enter the kingdom of heaven" (Matthew 5:20). Segundo also refers to this verse: "Why do you ask me about what is good? There is only one who is good. If you would enter life, keep the commandments" (Matthew 19:17). Segundo (1973, 2:140) then concludes, "Thus fulfillment of God's commands is both possible and necessary."[4]

Augustine's innovation was that grace is from God, and it is a force in the heart of the believer to behave righteously. As to righteousness, it is a life based on love. Love is reciprocal; we all dance. When we all dance, we create a loving community. Grace is always relational in nature. Our community is virtuous; we do selfless things. Virtues take love from an abstract idea to concrete actions. Our acceptance of each other is not condescending, like the rich giving alms to the poor and outcasts. The dance is transformative and makes the outcast part of the community. We are accepted into a community because grace has made us loveable; it has transformed us. Grace is not acceptance and a new identity. Grace is a force within which makes us willing and able to please God and thus be acceptable. Because we are

---

[4] Segundo was a universalist, believing that all humanity does good works. Thus, all of humanity has grace and is saved (Segundo 1973, 2:103). Setting that aside—and that is no small thing to set aside—Segundo clarifies that good works are an important feature of salvation.

changing, God accepts us, and others like being around us—thus, we belong. Welcome to Rainbow World, where we all dance.

Trying to Explain Gravity and Grace

The problem with gravity is that it is everywhere, all the time. All of us live in gravity, and only a few study gravity. The same is true of grace. When one studies their experience with grace, they gain an understanding about grace. Roger Haight (1979, 35) observes that Augustine tried to explain his conversion, his transformation, which was a phenomenon. Most of us just accept gravity; only a few study it. Augustine studied his grace experience through a theological microscope. Aquinas, Jansen, Luther, Calvin, and others studied Augustine's theology to understand grace. The basis of Augustine's observation was what he had experienced in his life and saw in scripture. If we want to talk about salvation and how it works (and not everyone needs or wants to do that), we should talk about grace from a "microscopic" perspective.

Pelagius, in an odd way, was also looking at grace. He just did not know that grace was what he was looking at. He realized that as a Christian, as well as a monk, he was able to overcome sinful desires. Look at Luther's commitment and personal sacrifice to his faith. He experienced grace. His life was enthusiastic for God, which he attributed to faith. But it was his faith that brought grace, the source of his enthusiasm. I think you get the picture; grace is pervasive. Where there is surrender (see Chapter 6), there is a flood of grace. Wherever there is mass, there is always gravity. You do not have to know anything about physics to experience gravity, and you do not have to know anything about theology to experience grace. As Pelagius demonstrated by his pietistic life, we can have terrible theology and still experience grace. Neither grace nor gravity has to be fully understood for it to work.

Paul illustrated with his Damascus Road conversion that a person can totally change their direction in life within a few days. In fact, grace can move a person in the opposite direction their life was headed. As others attest, this change in direction can happen in a moment. It is so dramatic and so personal, this change of heart, that it feels like a new birth.

Augustine and Aquinas were theological scientists. They dissected salvation in order to understand it. However, salvation also works for those who have no interest in dissecting theology. And the beauty of grace is that it is no respecter of persons. It works in the hearts of the surrendered, despite their social, educational, economic, cultural, or intellectual capacity.

The fruit of grace is expressions of selfless love, displayed by giving honor and praise to others. The consequences of grace are behaviors that produce a fellowship, community, belonging, acceptance, intimacy, and communion. When virtues produce a selfless community, the Kingdom of God is in full trinitarian bloom. Grace does this in ways that most Christians never understand. They just know something happened, and they have changed. We dance; indeed, because of grace, we must dance. When one is given the heart of a dancer, they can do nothing other than dance. The funny thing is that they may not even know why they are dancing.

⌘

Grace is a force that converts the human heart, and it is a force that pushes the Christian to continue to change throughout their life (sanctification). If grace can change us, then where do we go to get grace? In the next chapter, we will look at how to get grace.

5. Salvation: Starting the Dance

Grace went to war against the passion to be selfish and self-centered.

Church history tells a story about different ways to activate grace. Sadly, this history often contains criminal charges, punishment and even death for those who had different theological ideas. When Saul fell to his face on the Damascus Road, hearing the voice of God, he quickly experienced grace. His life dramatically changed. Similar to a bolt of lightning illuminating the night sky, God's grace in the life of Saul was an amazing and lightning-fast transformation from darkness to light. Theologians ask, what started this grace-motivated roar of transformation? We see changed lives all around us. Obviously, grace comes from God, but how do we connect to this force? When looking at the Big Bang, physicists can only look back and interpret the aftermath as a way to understand the present universe. The same with grace: theologians look at scriptures and their experiences of change and try to understand how transformation happens. The church and its theologians have considered many questions. But it all comes down to one question: what is the spark that starts the dance?

Politics is Hard on Theology

Before looking at some ideas about where to get grace, we need to take a moment to appreciate the Christian Church of the first 1,600 years. Christianity was born under the oppression of Roman imperialism. Rome and Greece had their own polytheistic religions. They were similar in that their religions were a geopolitical partnership between religion and the state. The state was the sponsor of religion. The amazing temples built by Rome and Greece were government projects. Religion legitimized the state by proclaiming those in power were approved and blessed by the gods to rule. Emperors, at times in history, were recognized by their citizens as gods. There was no separation of religious faith and political power. In this arrangement, the military and judicial powers of the state were at the disposal of religious leaders. War, conquest, and expansion became a religious expression. And religious purity, coupled with nationalism and allegiance to the king (or emperor), became a matter of the state. Religious faith and national loyalty were inseparable.

In the fourth century, because of the emperor Constantine, Christianity was accepted as a religion of Rome. Augustine realized the importance of the geopolitical framework of religion and state, which Rome had maintained over the centuries. He believed that a church and state partnership would help the Church Christianize the world (Bosch 2011, loc. 5705). Once Christianity was accepted by Rome, it became infused with political and judicial power. Later in history, the Spanish conquistadors were an example of the Church and state in partnership to conquer and Christianize the world.

When one reads church history, especially the first 1,600 years of the Church, one sees theological debates turn into jail time or execution for the losers. When the Church proclaimed a person or group to be heretics, the consequence was civil and criminal punishment. The Protestant Reformation was not only a theological break with the Roman Church; it was also a break from the geopolitical control of the Roman Church (Thomas 2020, 3–4). As a result, the early Protestants often had to hide or flee for their lives once they criticized the Roman Catholic Church.

Another reason for the Protestant Reformation was that many European states tried to free themselves from Rome's control. By adopting Protestantism, they could escape the political control of the Pope and his Church's armies. One example was Henry VIII and England's rejection of the Catholic Church. Unfortunately, many of these new Protestant states retained the church and state structure and used it to control the new Protestants. This political pressure was one reason that the religious refugees, the Pilgrims, migrated to the Americas to escape political control exerted on their religious faith. As one reads about theology and different theological camps, keep in mind the geopolitical reality of the church and state. Politics and civil governments have had a significant impact on what were deemed acceptable Christian beliefs.

The Church Saves

The theology of the sixteenth-century Roman Catholic Church was that the Roman Church was the bride of Christ and had the keys to the Kingdom. In the mind of the Roman Catholic Church, its sacraments were agents of grace. The concept was that grace, salvation and the sacraments were inseparable. A major controversy arose when the Roman Catholic Church did a fund-raising campaign to build St. Peter's Basilica in Rome. The Roman Church used its theological understanding of grace and rituals to promote a fund-raising strategy. Martin Luther, a Roman Catholic priest, stated his objection in the 82nd article of his thesis, the one he nailed to a German church door in 1517.

There are seven sacraments in the Roman Catholic Church, all of which are considered sources of grace (Kennedy 1912). All of these sacraments involve a priest conducting a ritual. The idea that developed was that there was a connection between the church's rituals and salvation. Saving grace was obtained through the church—in particular, the church's sacraments. This reasoning eventually led to a perversion of grace. The idea developed that the church could sell grace. If a person gave a generous donation, grace could be bought. It was a logical deduction. If the church is entrusted with the Kingdom and the Kingdom functions by grace, and if the sacraments are rituals of grace, then the church can distribute grace as it sees fit—in this case, through its rituals. In the name of fund-raising, grace was sold; the products sold were called *indulgences*.

Indulgences were certificates that said the church had given grace to the sinner; thus, salvation was obtained. The concept of indulgences is strongly related to identity grace. Buying grace, a certificate from the church, granted one a new Christian identity. Indulgences had little to do with a changed life. Indulgences were even sold for the long departed. Saving grace could be given to the dead—for the right price. In addition to raising money, this theology also kept civil and religious leaders in submission to the Roman Church. Excommunication involved removal from the church and its rituals and resulted in losing one's identity as a Christian.

Thus, Roman Catholic protesters, called Protestants, challenged the church, and eventually separated from it. In many cases, the Protestants (Martin Luther) were excommunicated by the Roman Catholic Church, thus losing their salvation in the eyes of the Roman Catholic Church. But the Protestants were not terribly worried about excommunication since they believed in faith-based grace. Luther believed that the Catholic Church could not give saving grace through the sacraments, but only by faith.

The connection of theology and political power in the Church's history impacted the development of theology. It is hard to imagine in this modern day that one's belief that grace came by faith and not a certificate could lead to jail time. Such was the world for pastors, priests, and theologians for many centuries.

Luther and other protesters became enemies of the church and state because they challenged the Catholic Church's view of how to acquire grace. The protesters proclaimed that the church could not give grace; only faith in Christ could lead to grace.

Self-Discipline Saves

For Pelagius, salvation is an act of the will; a person just has to want it. And if they want it, they can achieve it. This concept is no different than the ideas of self-determination that we see all around us. There is a cultural idea that if one tries hard enough and works hard enough, they can achieve anything. This mentality is Pelagianism. A famous shoemaker says it best: "Just do it!" In this framework, we all have the ability to do anything, find God, and live holy lives. Because of this, disciples of Pelagius believed in asceticism, self-discipline, self-denial, and restraint (Haight 1979, 36).

Pelagianism is found in many churches, often unknowingly practiced. The idea is that if one believes hard enough, with total sincerity, having no doubts, he or she can achieve or acquire whatever they imagine. Human effort brings us to God, holiness, and prosperity. In this case, the passion for changing is considered a human effort, not a gift from God. The incentive to change does not come from freedom and passion; it comes from the motive to succeed by being focused and disciplined. The Pelagian view is that we can succeed by our own efforts. Hard work brings change, which results in righteousness, success, and recognition. The motive behind the works is a quest for success and gaining prestige. As stated earlier, our human nature is always looking for others to honor us. Hard work and success are one way to gain honor for ourselves.

For the sake of visualization, the Pelagian idea is a person walks into Rainbow World and uses self-discipline to dance. These are martial arts dancers. They apply themselves, take control of their will, and force themselves to dance. Dancing is an effort of willing oneself to dance. Think of this as a Russian school of ballet. The student must practice, sweat, suffer, be disciplined, and then he or she will become a good dancer. Fame and fortune come to those who work hard. Therefore, salvation comes to those who work hard and gain recognition and a position of status. In this context, the hope for success is the motivator. We dance, but only because we want to stand on the stage and be acknowledged as extraordinary. Works are based on fame. Dancing is not about building community; it is about standing out and being recognized. Our righteousness is motivated by pride. From this perspective success confirms God's favor and acceptance. The faithful are prosperous and the most faithful are the most prosperous.

Our Two Natures

Living in sin is living without grace. Sin does what sin does: it creates pleasure in "self" and causes conflict, alienation, and isolation. This is our human nature. Adam and Eve once walked with God in the garden; after sin they walked alone. Humans are social beings, created in God's image to be social. The result of sin is loneliness. Humanity, using all its human intellect and energy, tries to regain community. One approach to community is to gain acceptance. Change can be motivated by seeking the acceptance of others. We do what makes others accept us. We dance based on how everyone expects us to dance, hoping they will accept us. Yet Augustine challenged the idea of forcing oneself to dance for the reward of acceptance. Dancing should be natural, or as

Aquinas said, supernatural.[5] Forced dancing, even for acceptance by others, is a false grace. We are dancing for the wrong reason.

For example, Adam and Eve lived righteously. They delighted in living righteously. They liked to dance; it was enjoyable. There was no need to give them a prize to do something they loved doing. Their dancing was not an attempt to be accepted. It was who they were and produced, as a consequence, acceptance. They were loving, and, true to genuine love, they were not seeking to gain something from those they loved. There was no pride or shame in their relationship. Adam and Eve, before the Fall, lived by grace. Their dance was genuine because it was not self-seeking. Acceptance was what they gave, not what they expected.

Augustine explained that there was always the potential for Adam and Eve to sin. Grace did not make Adam and Eve unable to sin; it made them not desire sin. It was their nature to be righteous. Grace gave them the ability to avoid sin, but they could still be tempted to sin (Vanderschaaf 1976, 1–2). They were virtuous. Augustine said grace was God's nature in Adam and Eve. They were loving and they were freely loving.

Augustine presented the idea of "nothingness." Before creation, there was nothing. In the absence of God's grace, humans move toward isolation and oblivion. God does not destroy the sinner so much as the sinner destroys him or herself. They do this by sinfulness, which increases our alienation from God and others. By their own wills, their human nature, they

---

[5] The Spanish Dominican Domingo Báñez, in the sixteenth century, challenged the idea that the passion of grace was supernatural. Rather, he believed it was natural. Christians lived a virtuous life by grace, which was their original state in the Garden of Eden. Their natural state was virtuous (O'Callaghan 2016, 205). That said, the terms may be different, but the ideas of Aquinas and Báñez are similar. Adam and Eve lived by grace, and grace produced and continues to produce a virtuous life.

return to the time before creation—to an empty void. Both Augustine and Aquinas believed that Adam and Eve had the freedom to stop dancing. Sin, which was a decision of Adam and Eve, diminished God's grace, and selfishness became humanity's new passion. The consequence, explained Augustine, was that humanity started a march to nothingness. "In so far as creation is made out of nothing it retains the inherent tendency to fall away from God to nothingness" (Vanderschaaf 1976, 3). Nothingness is not a cosmic void for humans; it is aloneness, which is the consequence of selfishness. That does not mean that the desperately alone person is content to be alone—no, although unchanged and without virtues, they fight a futile fight to be accepted.

Adam and Eve, after the Fall, ended up with two things: the shadow of divine nature and the formidable human sin nature. This was God's warning. If they disobeyed, they would know good and evil. To know evil is to know our self-serving human desires and to experience the consequence of those desires. God knows about evil, but God is not evil. Humans, after the Fall, discovered what God knew. Evil leads to behaviors that break relationships and result in isolation. All humans have the shadow of divine nature and are infected with a sinful nature. Sickness always overpowers health. The unconverted sinner is so tightly held in the bonds of their human nature that they feel imprisoned and alone.

In the case of living by grace in the Garden of Eden, Adam and Eve were not trapped as prisoners in grace. Adam and Eve always had free will, before and after the Fall. The same is true of their descendants. Initially, human nature was selfless, worshipful of God, and honoring of each other. In the Garden of Eden, humans were in the image and nature of God. Then sin came, and human passions changed. After sin, the sinner was a prisoner to selfishness and pride. They had known the passion to do good; now they knew evil. God said they would know evil; they would know what it feels like to be powerless.

After the Fall and faith in Christ, grace went to war against the passion to be selfish and self-centered. Through faith in Christ, an act of the will, the believer starts a fight against sin. Grace (desires for things that please God) goes to war with the desires of the flesh (selfishness and self-centeredness). In a real sense, grace starts a war. This was God's warning in the Garden of Eden: if you eat the forbidden fruit humanity will live with both the knowledge of good and evil (Genesis 3). Humans are in a war of passions. Grace goes to war with our selfish human passions.

Seeking acceptance from others by using our self-discipline, on the other hand, put us in an unwinnable war against an unwilling will. The non-Christian is in a hopeless battle trying to use self-discipline to fight off the selfish passions that imprison and isolate him or her. Humanity knows what it feels like to be powerless to change. To know the inability to escape our destructive passions is to know evil. Paul puts it this way: "But I see in my members another law waging war against the law of my mind and making me captive to the law of sin that dwells in my members. Wretched man that I am! Who will deliver me from this body of death?" (Romans 7:23-24). Grace, on the other hand, goes to war on the very ground on which sin gained victory. It changes the heart from selfish to selfless. Grace implants a new passion, a competitor. There are two natures, natural and supernatural, and grace is the supernatural force of change.

Human Responsibility: Grace Given by God to The Chosen

There are two views about a person's responsibility with respect to receiving grace. One camp maintains that grace is given, and the other, that grace must be accepted.[6] Although they are the same experience of delight, the two sides are different. First, we will look at grace as a power from God that flows over the believer. Second, in the next section, we will look at a contrasting view that grace comes into the believer's life based on something they do. In both cases, dancers dance.

Augustine believed that God touches some people and they are gifted grace (Augustine 2010, ch. 43). Aquinas (1991, ch. 2, vol. 23:3), harmonizing with Augustine, stated that predestination did not take away a person's free will. His explanation was that any person could come to faith, but they would not do so without grace. Aquinas's remarkable insight was that the freedom to choose and chosen-ness were simultaneous. John Calvin, a student of Augustinian ideas, took Augustine's ideas and went a different direction. His emphasis was not on free will, but on God's sovereignty. God selects some to salvation, but not everyone. The issue is no longer free will, but God's sovereign act of selection. God is in total control, and humans control nothing. Grace is given to those God selects; once selected, their passions bend toward pleasing God.

Augustine and Aquinas emphasized the importance of free will. As Aquinas explained, selection and surrender are a simultaneous event. However, Augustine, Aquinas, and even

---

[6] There are two distinguishable characteristics of grace. One is "sufficient" grace, which leaves space for human response. And the other is "efficacious" or "operative" grace, which brings about in humans what God wants (O'Callaghan 2016, 201). Calvinist Protestants refer to efficacious grace as irresistible grace.

Calvin understood grace as an explosion of new godly desires and abilities that diminished natural cravings and wrongdoings and instilled delight in godliness.

Augustine and those who followed him, including Aquinas, Jansen, and Calvin, were all pretty clear on who would receive grace. God selected those to whom God gifted grace. Aquinas, reflecting Augustine, explains that there is nothing the sinner did to merit grace. At the same time, Aquinas explains that the sinner has the free will to renounce sin. Aquinas understands free will and God's sovereignty like wheels on a bicycle: unless there are two, the bicycle does not function. God allows the sinner to do what they want to do. Therefore, their reprobation is not God's fault; it is the sinner's fault. Aquinas is trying to protect God's reputation. God is not at fault for humanity's sin. By focusing on human free will, humankind becomes responsible for their sins. Aquinas (1991, ch. 2, vol. 23:1-4) states, "The reprobate-as-such cannot acquire grace, but of his own free will he lands himself in this or that sin and that can rightly be called his fault."

In the case of Rainbow World and the Aquinas concept, a person decides to enter Rainbow World, and, at that precise moment, they are selected by God. The person chooses to join, and he or she is infused with a passion and the ability to dance at that moment. By making the two events simultaneous, Aquinas protects the idea of grace as a changing force we can activate by repentance. By combining free will and God's selection as a singular event, God is not the author of sin. Rather, we are free to repent and experience grace, and God is in full control.

Human Responsibility: Grace Offered by God and Accepted

Now to the other side of the grace coin. Not all Roman Catholics or Protestants believed grace was imposed on a selected group by God. Instead, some promoted the idea that grace was universally available to all people and was only to be accepted.

One of the contemporaries of the Protestant reformer Martin Luther was a Dutch priest, Erasmus of Rotterdam. Erasmus was sympathetic to many of the concerns of the Protestant reformation, but he remained in the Roman Catholic Church. He agreed with many of Luther's ideas, but he held a different view about grace. Erasmus believed in a type of partnership between humanity and God. For the sake of illustration, let us say humankind lives in darkness because humans close their eyes and choose to live in darkness. God lights up the world. Grace and righteousness are the light that bathes the blind sinner. However, the sinner must partner with God and open their eyes. The sinner's part is simply to open their eyes. Thus, says Erasmus, the sinner has free will and can choose to accept God's grace. God has done almost everything, but the sinner only has to open their eyes and be filled with light (Cheah 1995).

Erasmus was not a Pelagianist, because he believed that God's grace empowered transformation, not human effort. Erasmus believed that the sinner had control over their destiny. The sinner could repent, profess faith in Christ, and receive God's grace. The sinner was not incapable of opening their eyes to see. Luther, like Calvin, believed the sinner was hopeless and powerless to do anything to bring grace into their life. God had to do everything, and God selected some to receive grace and not others. In contrast, Erasmus looked to 1 Corinthians 3:9-10 to explain the partnership: "For we are God's fellow workers. You are God's field, God's building. According to the grace of God given to me, like a skilled master builder I laid a foundation, and someone else is building upon it. Let each one take care how he builds upon it." The Greek uses the word *synergoi* for "fellow workers." The English word *synergy* is derived from this Greek word.

Erasmus's idea was similar to that of the Eastern Orthodox Church. The Orthodox promote the idea of "synergy" (fellow workers)—that is, that God and humankind could be partners. The Eastern Orthodox understanding of synergism states that "humans beings always have the freedom to choose, in their personal (gnomic) wills, whether to walk with God or turn from Him", but "what God does is incomparably more important than what we humans do" (Payton 2007, 151). God does God's part, which is significant, but humans must do their small part. The sinner has the ability to open their eyes, and then God floods their hearts with grace.

John Wesley was the Protestant that took this idea to the masses. Wesley was neither a Calvinist nor a predestinarian. He taught that there were three aspects of grace. He believed that God's grace was prevenient. That is, there is a slight "intimation" for God in all humans. In all of creation, one finds God's grace. In the soul of all humans is an attraction or an interest in God. Augustine agreed with this idea. Wesley explained that this introductory grace prepared one for salvation. When one hears the gospel message, he or she is awakened to their sinfulness. They become aware of their selfish and shameful behaviors. The sinner then compares their life to God's moral law, which is a general sense of right and wrong (Knight 2018, 51).

Prevenient grace is a type of grace given to all, and its purpose is to call all humanity to repentance. This grace is universal, which means there is a dissatisfaction that all humans have about their lives. Something is not right, and everyone knows it. Prevenient grace is a God-given curiosity or desire to change and to know more about God. This concept is consistent with Erasmus's idea of grace: God prepares all of humankind to see, but each must open their own eyes.

The second aspect of grace for Wesley was saving grace. This act of grace comes from repentance and God's forgiveness. Wesley did not think like the revivalist, which involved simply an altar call and instant conversion. He saw repentance as a process that took time and discipleship. For Westley, conversion takes more time for some than others, and grace grows in the heart at different speeds in different people (Knight 2018, 53). Eventually, he believed, grace would take control of the will, producing salvation. At some point grace grows to a level in which one changes and wants to live for Christ.

Wesley's third aspect of grace was sanctifying grace. God wants us to be like Christ, and God gives us the power to change into the image of Christ. Wesley's idea was that grace changed one's heart. Grace resulted in changing one's life, a continual process called sanctification (Carder 2016).

Wesley believed that a person, after receiving grace, could resist God and lose God's grace. In other words, they would return to the experience of prevenient grace, but not justifying or sanctifying grace. This understanding meant that a person's faith and salvation could be lost without a holy and changed life. In Wesley's theology of grace, sanctifying grace (living holy lives) affirmed one's salvation. Obviously, this perspective produced a challenge. How holy does one have to be to be holy enough? Followers of Wesley were expected not to do evil and to do good. They were to demonstrate their conversion through acts of godliness (Carder 2016). Grace, for Wesley, is like a lake filling up with water. At some point the water becomes high enough in the lake to generate power in a dam. But if the water goes down, the force stops.

In the case of Wesley's theology, everyone has self-awareness. Their level of interest in God is their decision. Once a person expresses faith in Christ, God gives them a passion for dancing. They dance, and it affirms their faith in Christ. But if they lose interest in dancing, they have lost their faith. They can walk out of Rainbow World and not dance anymore, and consequently, they are no longer dancers.

Interestingly, in the early 1800s, in the shadow of the Second Great Awakening, a group of Presbyterians in the USA combined Calvin and Wesley's ideas to form a middle ground. These Presbyterian pastors were participants in the evangelistic camp meetings and saw thousands profess faith in Christ. As a result, they adjusted their theology to conform to their reality. These Presbyterian pastors were members of Cumberland Presbytery in Kentucky. The Presbyterian Church became increasingly uneasy with the revivalists and insisted their pastors refrain from participation in the camp meetings. The camp meetings were emotional and controversial. These Cumberland Presbytery ministers refused to renounce the Great Awakening. Their continued participation resulted in the formation of non-predestinarian Presbyterians, called the Cumberland Presbyterian Church.

The Cumberland Presbyterians were advocates of a new medium theology, a "who-so-ever-will" theology ("Confession of Faith and Government for Cumberland Presbyterians" 1984, iii). Their theology was similar to Erasmus and the Orthodox synergist. Erasmus was also characterized as promoting a medium theology (Cheah 1995). However, the Cumberlands did not go as far as Wesley. Consistent with the revivalists, salvation and grace happened at a moment in time, for example, an altar call. Once one came to Christ, the Cumberlands believed that their salvation was assured. It could not be lost. The Cumberlands believed that through repentance, God gave grace, and the grace given was owned by God. From the Cumberland view, the believer could not give away what was not theirs. Consistent with Erasmus, the Cumberlands believed that the sinner opened their eyes (repentance is an act of the will), received light (an act of God), and never knew blindness again (God preserves the believer) ("Confession of Faith and Government for Cumberland Presbyterians" 1984, 10).

Grace Through the Sacraments

Augustine believed that baptism gave grace to infants by removing original sin and to adults by removing original sin and sins they had committed (G. R. Lewis and Demarest 1996, bk. 3, pg. 74). He connected sacraments to grace. Aquinas (1991, ch. 15, vol. 62:1) clearly believed that the sacraments were a source of grace and could help Christians be better people—that is, to change. Aquinas (1991, ch. 15, vol. 61:2) also believed that grace allowed the Christian to share in God's likeness (identity), and the sacraments were a visible way to identify with Christ. Aquinas (1991, ch. 15, vol. 69:2) said, "Baptism has the power to remove even the inherited defects of our present life, but that power takes effect not in the present life but only when just men rise again." In an earlier section of this chapter, I explained the abuse of the sacraments by the Catholic Church. However, the ideas before indulgences are worth study.

For Aquinas, baptism was not sinlessness; baptism conveyed our new identity and future hope. In fact, at baptism, it was common to select a new Christian name, a new identity. In the case of infants, they were named—that is, given a Christian identity—at their baptism. Aquinas explained that the sacraments do two things concerning grace. First, they remove punishments, which were the result of our sins, and we are made righteous (a new identity). And second, they gave one strength to live a Christian life (through a force within) (1991, ch. 15, vol. 61:5). Aquinas (1991, ch. 15 vol. 65:1) stated that the church has seven sacraments intended to give humankind the disposition to worship God and "remedy the effects of sin." The sacraments were a force for change.

In addition to the ability of the sacrament to change us, Augustine and Aquinas understood their church to be the only church. The Roman Catholic Church, throughout history, has explained that salvation comes from the church. The early church father Origen declared, "Outside the Church nobody will be saved" (Hardon 1981, 234). Both Augustine and Aquinas believed there could be extraordinary circumstances in which a person could be saved outside the church, but by and large, salvation was the church's role (Hardon 1981, 235).

As the Catholic Catechism explains, incorporation into the Church is by the Church's sacraments (Hardon 1981, 236). This concept became a flashpoint for the Protestants. Salvation, said the protesters, was separate from the Church and her sacraments. Protestants referred to the rituals of the Roman Catholic Church and its sacraments, including indulgences, as "works."

Look at the sacraments this way: if one wanted to join Rainbow World, there was an initiation process. That process, said the Catholic Church, involved the ritual of Baptism. There was only one place to get a ticket to enter Rainbow World, and that was by baptism in the Catholic Church. Once in Rainbow World, if one wanted to dance better, then the Church's rituals would provide the passion and the skills to be a better dancer. As noted in the prior chapter, that concept caused some in the church to "charge" money to enter Rainbow World. That mistake created a fracture that led to the birth of Protestant churches and a new examination of grace.

Martin Luther was close to Augustine and Aquinas concerning the sacraments. In his view, the sacraments had power in that they were able to sanctify but not save. In Luther's mind, faith combined with the sacraments produced grace. John Calvin was also in line with Augustine, Aquinas, and Luther. Calvin believed that salvation was a consequence of faith, in agreement with Luther. In other words, neither Luther nor Calvin thought the water, bread, or wine in the hands of the Church produced salvation. However, Luther and Calvin believed that faith in Christ and the Lord's Supper would cause a spiritual interaction that would produce change. Interestingly, Calvin focused on the community aspect of the Lord's Supper. Communion was intended to produce mutual love among Christians and inspire gratitude and worship for God. Protestants began to use the word communion, or Holy Communion, in place of the word "Eucharist." As a result, believed Calvin, the Lord's Supper should be taken each week. The shift was from sacraments that save to sacraments that stimulate a loving community.

Another view of the Protestants was from a man named Ulrich Zwingli, a Swiss Protestant. He posed that the sacraments were only symbolic. This symbolic understanding of the sacraments is widely held by Protestants today. Zwingli believed that the sacraments had no power to change believers. They were a visual object lesson. The sacraments did not increase one's desire to be godly.

Keep in mind that Augustine and Aquinas believed that God chooses the dancers, and the sacraments are part of their election. Salvation, election, free will, and receiving the sacraments are all simultaneous. The emphasis on simultaneity protected free will and God's sovereignty, and it also protected God from being blamed for humanity's sin. As for living righteously, by taking the sacraments, one becomes more righteous. For some theologians, even Protestants, there is power in the sacraments. Once we start dancing, the sacraments help us dance better. Thus, the sacraments are understood to be a source of change.

For Luther and Calvin (G. R. Lewis and Demarest 1996, bk. 3, pp. 247–52), faith (which God gives to some) came first, and the sacraments (baptism and the Lord's Supper) were part of the Christian's walk. They were a source of Christian growth. Luther and Calvin believed that the sacraments had the power to change a person for the better. The church was a community that related with God and each other better because of the sacraments. God gifts faith and grace, and we dance. Once we start dancing, the sacraments help us dance better.

Salvation Defined by the Human Experience with Grace

As people tell about their experience with salvation, they define grace. One's experience with God, when told, reveals the force of grace. As noted earlier, one sees a common pattern if one looks at these theologians from purely an experiential perspective. They are all trying to explain their experience. Augustine described the salvation experience as an experience of grace. The common denominator from Christians as they told their stories was that they were changed.

Authentic change is based on the want (will) and the ability to be different than we are. The diversity of ideas around grace resulted from different Christians trying to answer the questions that this experience provoked. The real issue for these early theologians, both Catholic and Protestant, was the acquisition of grace and the management of grace. They all knew from experience that grace was powerful and transformative, and they were all trying to figure it out. Their theological explanations were like a physicist making declarations about gravity in hopes that their daily experience with gravity would help them understand it and better use it.

The critical point is all these questions are focused on one thing, which is trying to understand a transformative conversion experience. If we can look at the experience as our starting point, then we might better understand this passion to change. The following are the brief change stories of several mentioned in this book who studied grace.

Augustine's youth was characterized as undisciplined. His mother was a Christian; his father, a successful non-Christian Roman (who later converted to Christianity). Augustine received a great education in public speaking. Augustine lived with his girlfriend, a relationship initiated in their teens. He characterized his youth as immoral and explored religious ideas to bring peace to his anxieties about sin and God. As a young teacher of public speaking in Milan, he attended the preaching of the Bishop of Milan, Aurelius Ambrose. Ambrose was known for his eloquent speaking style. One of Ambrose's sermons impacted Augustine. Not long after hearing the sermon, Augustine offered to house-sit with a friend. History records that he and his friend were in the house's garden. Augustine writes how he was in great distress about his life. He was frustrated, emotional, and perplexed about God. He heard a child chanting a song that he interpreted as God's message to open the Bible and read it. He opened the Bible to Romans 13:13-14. These verses were explicitly focused on carousing, drunkenness, sexual immorality, quarreling, and jealousy. Augustine saw himself in those verses. Then Paul, in the verses of Romans, instructed those he addressed to put on Jesus Christ and deny their flesh. Augustine, who had been living a life of decadence, thought God was talking to him. Augustine explained he felt that his heart had been flooded with light. He turned his life around and was baptized in 387 AD. He later noted that until his heart had found Christ, he had not known peace.

Aquinas's conversion was not as dramatic as Augustine's conversation, but his resilience speaks deeply of his commitment. Thomas Aquinas was the son of influential Italian parents. They sent him to school, anticipating he would be educated and become an official in the church. While in his teens, studying in Naples, he was influenced by the teaching of a Dominican teacher who stressed the monastic life, study, and preaching. Dominicans also maintained high moral standards. Aquinas decided he wanted to be a Dominican monk. His family reacted to his decision to be a monk by locking him in a castle for over a year, hoping he would reconsider. He did not and moved to Paris to study theology with the Dominicans. He became one of the great theologians of Christianity. He was a student and later teacher of Augustinian theology.

Little is known of Pelagius. He was probably from Ireland or England, although he lived in Rome for many years. Those who knew him, even his adversaries, said he was highly educated and well versed in theology. Pelagius was never ordained a priest. He was a monk and lived an austere life as a layman. Augustine, who strongly disagreed with Pelagius, called him a "saintly man."

John Calvin did not share his conversion story, but he did refer to making a change in his life. Calvin was the last of four children. His father was successful enough to send him to Paris to be educated. The initial plan was that Calvin would be a priest. Later his father decided he should be a lawyer. John Calvin studied law and was licensed as a lawyer. He continued to study religion and was particularly interested in Augustinian theology. He reported that at some point, he became dissatisfied with the Roman Catholic Church. Amid his disillusionment, he reported that "this mere taste of true godliness that I received set me on fire with such a desire to progress that I pursued the rest of my [Roman Catholic] studies more coolly, although I did not give them up altogether" (Bouwsma 1988, 10). There were complaints in Paris about the Roman Catholic Church and the need for reforms. Calvin was implicated as sympathetic to the reform movement and, as a result, had to flee Paris. Eventually, Calvin joined this group of dissatisfied protesters. He became a leader of Protestant Reformed theology and developed the theological and polity basis of Presbyterianism.

Martin Luther was a German ordained priest, teacher, and student of Augustinian theology. He was the child of common workers. His father sent him to school to be a lawyer. Luther finished his education in the least amount of time a student could graduate; he was brilliant. As a twenty-one year old, he was traveling in a thunderstorm when a bolt of lightning hit close to him, resulting in a spiritual awakening. He surrendered to the ministry and started studies to be a priest and monk. Luther was a very devout monk, fasting, praying, studying, and demonstrating aesthetic practices of self-denial and self-imposed suffering. His studies lead to a doctorate and a professorship. While teaching the New Testament book of Romans, he realized that all his efforts to please God were in vain. What God required was faith, only faith in Christ. Within a few years after this new realization, representatives from the Roman Catholic Church arrived where Luther lived and started to sell indulgences. This action led to Luther's protest, and he published his objections, which he shared with others. From Luther's lightning bolt awakening to his studies on Romans, Luther demonstrated an intense passion for suffering and laboring for the cause of Christ.

John Wesley was from England and the son of devout Christian parents. John Wesley gained a master's degree, and then he became a teacher. He was ordained as an Anglican priest. Wesley took a break from teaching to dedicate himself to a deeper commitment to Christ. He practiced ascetic forms of spirituality. Wesley returned to the pastorate and joined forces with his brother Charles, who was also a priest. His brother had started discipleship groups within the church that emphasized greater commitment. John led a group, using many of the ascetic practices he had been using, and the group he led grew. This group was looked at with suspicion by others, and they were considered fanatical. John then made a trip to the American colonies. He was asked to pastor a church in Georgia. Several issues in Georgia made Wesley's time in Georgia complicated, so he resigned from his position and returned to England disappointed. Wesley attended a Moravian service, and while at the service, he had a spiritual awakening. He later interpreted the experience as a conversion experience. As a result of his experience, he began to preach Luther's idea of professing faith in Christ as the means to salvation. Wesley practiced evangelism that focused on professing one's faith and formed small discipleship groups that stressed personal commitment. These groups grew, and over time they resulted in the development of the Methodist Church.

Billy Graham, evangelist and revivalist of the twentieth century, is representative of many evangelicals. He speaks of his conversion, and conversion in general, as a personal relationship with Jesus Christ. He committed his life to a person, and that person was Jesus Christ. His spiritual awakening and commitment to Christ took place in a revival meeting when he was a teenager.

Concerning his conversion, Graham explained, "It would take some time before I understood what happened to me well enough to explain it to anybody else. There were signs, though, that my thinking and direction had changed, that I was truly converted. To my own surprise, church activities that had bored me before seemed interesting all of a sudden." He continued, "I actually wanted to go to church as often as possible" (Graham 1997, 31). Graham spoke of a new interest in the Bible and in prayer. His faith was intimate, passionate, and personal.

One could ask, "How does one have a 'relationship' with Jesus Christ, a person who walked the earth over 2,000 years ago?" The very nature of grace is that grace is a personal experience. One's will becomes God's will. One can feel the change taking place. The feeling of grace is one of freedom, not an obligation. Grace creates a desire to change, like a hunger for a favorite food. It is a feeling of freedom, and a sense of God's presence in our hearts. It is personal, real and powerful. Grace is beyond human formation or invention—at times even beyond the human ability to describe it. Grace is forming us; we are not inventing it. Grace is our encounter with God. In the case of salvation, it is our first encounter.

The Spark That Starts Change

The account of Paul on the Damascus Road and the above stories show some common patterns related to grace. In each case, there was an awakening. The father of psychology, Dr. William James (2011, 165), a Harvard professor, wrote a book on religious experience. In his research, which one could characterize as a qualitative study of human religious behavior, he examined the conversion experience. He noted that sometimes something happens in a person's mind and what were once minor ideas take central place and become a source of energy. He called it the hot place of their consciousness, a *centre* of personal energy.

As a scientist and psychologist, Dr. James believed that this energy came as a result of surrender. A person, possibly because of a life crisis, or because they were frustrated that their life was far from ideal, gave up. He said they relaxed in helplessness. This act of yielding, he explained, allowed a new force to arise and open their mind to ideas that were once minor, thus becoming enthusiastic about those ideas (James 2011, 174–76).

The above examples reference a moment of brokenness, resulting in a flood of new energy. Dr. James (2011, 193) believed that the moment of surrender allowed the subconscious mind to break through and flower into a burst of maturity. He then observed that this flowering of maturity took on the form of sanctity. This energy produced emotions and passion, which drove godliness. One's mind and life opened to the reality of a personal God; one became willing to surrender control to God, love, unity, and selflessness (James 2011, 223). This excitement is what the aforementioned Christian leaders called *grace.* Even the scientist William James referred to this psychological phenomenon as a force of "grace."

The starting point for change is brokenness. James (2011, 177) noted that even if a person tries to will themselves to live a better life, feel better, or stop doing what leaves one feeling unfulfilled, the effort is in vain. The effort to believe and change only leaves one feeling hopeless, not better. As a result, the only way to find relief is to surrender. James (2011, 147) explained that this moment of surrender could be sudden for some people, and with others, it could be gradual. Regardless of the pace grace comes into a person's life, James believed that the entrance of grace was by surrender, and that grace was an external force that brought new energy.

The books of James and First Peter provide a basis for the spark which starts change. "But he gives more grace. Therefore, it says, 'God opposes the proud but gives grace to the humble.' Submit yourselves therefore to God. Resist the devil, and he will flee from you" (James 4:6-7). Peter says the same: "Likewise, you who are younger, be subject to the elders. Clothe yourselves, all of you, with humility toward one another, for 'God opposes the proud but gives grace to the humble.' Humble yourselves, therefore, under the mighty hand of God so that at the proper time he may exalt you" (1 Peter 5:5-6). Humility is the act of yielding, surrendering, giving up, and relaxing. Dr. William James believed surrender released the subconscious mind, which gave new values and direction in life. Christian leaders believed surrender produced grace, a force from the Holy Spirit that transformed a person. Once again, one can debate if the force is supernatural power (divine intervention) or hidden human consciousness (psychological realization), but both agree it comes from emotional brokenness. The spark of humility produces a flood of change.

Dr. James, as many of the above testimonials of conversion attest, spoke of a crisis or frustration with life as the spark that caused surrender. This crisis produced a spark of humility, which led to an experience of renewal. (In Chapter 6, we will talk about another response to the hardships in life that produces the opposite of grace.)

The scriptures also show another event that can cause humility. A miracle or an extraordinary event can have a profound impact on a person. In Luke 5, Jesus was preaching from a fisherman's boat to a crowd on the banks of Galilee. He and the fisherman pulled away from the shore, and Jesus spoke to the crowd on the riverbank. He instructed the fisherman to lower their nets. Their catch of fish was so large it damaged their nets.

Peter, who was one of the fishermen, responded, "I am a sinful man." Peter, James, and John, who were in the boat and experienced the miracle, became Jesus's followers. For whatever reason, this miraculous event had the same effect as a crisis: it humbled the fishermen, and they surrendered. They changed their direction in life, from fishermen to be fishers of men. Some people experience something so extraordinary that they are profoundly humbled.

In the context of gradual conversion, there is another experience that many Christians confirm. Some Christians have always felt converted, never knowing a time when they were not converted. Members of Christian families often share this type of faith testimonial. Ruth Graham, the wife of the famous American revivalist Billy Graham, remarked that she was raised by Presbyterian missionary parents and never knew a time when she did not have faith in Christ. However, all people in this category do speak of moments of crisis and frustration in their life. Even those that have always been surrounded by Christian belief and have always professed faith have moments of surrender and renewal. These moments made them feel closer to God and gave them greater motivation to serve God.

Conversion, its classical definition, is a change in direction which is neither forced nor coerced. The converted willfully change directions. As we have seen in prior explanations, the pleasure found in doing what one wills, which takes one in a new direction, is the force of God's grace. Grace is sparked by either a crisis, frustration with the status quo, or a miraculous event. All these experiences are humbling. Grace is ignited by humility and surrender. As the scientist William James implies, from a psychological perspective, one must first be empty before being filled. Paul affirms this idea in 2 Corinthians 12:9. In Paul's conversation with God, God said, "'My grace is sufficient for you, for my power is made perfect in weakness." Paul's analysis was, "Therefore I will boast all the more gladly of my weaknesses, so that the power of Christ may rest upon me."

⌘

The next chapter looks at grace as a dynamic force of change that builds upon itself like a snowball rolling downhill. Grace is not a one-time experience; it is a continual process of change that transforms our lives. This next chapter explores how to set our sails and ride the winds of grace.

6. Sanctification: The Motivation to Dance Well

Grace produced works that produced more grace and more works.

God's grace is a spark that starts a process. The process is sanctification. Grace to grace, which is to say, the grace that begins salvation, is the same grace that sustains salvation. Chapter 2 explained that grace has two parts: the actual side and the sanctifying side. Actual grace is God's gift of enthusiasm for godliness; this is salvation. It is God bestowing our new nature, our new heart, one that desires God. The sanctifying side of grace is focused on habits or virtues one develops as a result of grace. One has the appetite through grace to live a sacred routine. The passion Christians have to worship God and follow Christ as Lord is the same passion that promotes new attitudes and a new lifestyle. Roger Haight (1979, 154) explains that spirituality is the central focus of grace. Spirituality is enthusiasm for habits and disciplines that allow one to walk and talk as Christ walked and talked. Why is that important? Because Jesus was a member of the perfect community. We can develop a community by following the passions of grace. They allow us to think and live as Jesus did and relate to others as Jesus related to his Father.

By grace, one wants to be in Rainbow World. The converted person wants to join in on the dance. Once in Rainbow World, one wants to learn how to dance. The believer is enthusiastic about learning how to dance well. Grace is like eating ice cream in an ice cream shop. First is the desire to eat ice cream, which brings one into the door of the ice cream shop. Second is selecting the ice cream and toppings and then eating the ice cream. The two go together, but they are different experiences. The passion we have to dance leads to a passion for learning to dance. Grace gives us an enthusiasm for virtuous habits.

Grace Flows from Humility

The ancient Greeks negatively understood humility as a lower-class status, which involved low intellect. The humble were born humble by parentage; for the Greeks being humble was an inferior state of existence (Kittel and Friedrich 1972, VIII:2). The biblical understanding, on the other hand, was that humility was virtuous. Being humble was noble. It did not refer to a weak and flawed person; it referred to a considerate and unassuming person. Jesus exhorted his disciples that the path to greatness was to be like a child. "Whoever humbles himself like this child is the greatest in the kingdom of heaven" (Matthew 18:4). The idea was that for the disciple to be humble, he or she lowered him or herself. They were dependent on God, followers of Christ, and in service to others (Kittel and Friedrich 1972, VIII:16–17).

The English writer and theologian C.S. Lewis (2001, 127) stated, "For Pride is spiritual cancer: it eats up the very possibility of love, or contentment, or even common sense." For Lewis, pride destroyed community, peace, and intelligence. The proud are selfish, contentious, and simple-minded. Humility involves opening our hearts to hear. By hearing we learn about the ways of God.

Augustine (2007, 236–39) preached a sermon about Mary and Martha. He explained how Mary humbly sat and listened to Jesus teach. Martha, on the other hand, was a great host who was busy serving her guest. Jesus said, "Mary has chosen the good portion, which will not be taken away from her" (Luke 10:42). What humility gave Mary was lasting, not temporary like a glass of wine or a loaf of bread. Knowledge, which changes our lives, becomes possible when we are humble. Humility is to surrender, relax, listen, and learn. The humble are willing to be taught and to be led. Humility is not a "work" we do; it is an attitude of surrender. In a way, humility is the opposite of works. Mary did not work; she sat and listened. We surrender, and we are then transformed.

If grace were an explosive, humility would be the detonator. Grace starts through surrender. Surrender is the first act of the transformative power of humility. Humility continues the transformation of one's life. In a word, change is the result of humility. God gives grace to the humble.

Augustine (2014, ch. 5) stated the prominence of humility when he explained that God was made a man to demonstrate humility. God was born of a woman in a barn full of animals. God lived among angry and disrespectful people. God unjustly died on the cross as a criminal. Through these acts of humility, God cured humanity's sins. Humility is such a powerful tool that even God used it to break the back of sin. Humility is the first step towards selflessness and prepares the way for grace.

Karl Barth turns to the Trinity to illustrate humility. He explained that God both commands and expresses humility by obeying (Barth and Johnson 2019, 248). God demonstrated humility through the person of Jesus. Jesus was obedient to the Father. As Barth explained, God commanded, and God's son obeyed. Barth notes that the obedience of Jesus was God showing humility. Jesus was God incarnate (in the flesh). Thus, as Barth observed, God commanded, and God obeyed. Therefore, God was humble. Humility brings the wind that drives the ship on its redemptive journey. The force that saves starts with setting oneself aside.

Augustine understood humility as emptying. He used the analogy of a house that was cleaned out. He believed that the person that is converted to Christ must first be emptied. Then, explained Augustine, the Holy Spirit comes into the empty house. Augustine clearly understood "empty" to mean humble. Once the Holy Spirit moves in one's heart grace has its effect. "He fills and guides and leads the person, restrains from evil and spurs on to good, makes justice delightful, so that the person does good out of love for what is right" (Augustine 2007, 111 Sermon 72 A).

As the psychologist William James explained, a person seeking conversion must surrender their personal will. The person stops their efforts to go in the direction they desire to go. Dr. James explained that humility has two characteristics: the feeling of wrongness or dissatisfaction with the way things are, and the optimistic feeling that there is a way out of our discontent. Dr. James (2011, 174–75) noted that a person could have a vision of a positive ideal that was obtainable. To break from dissatisfaction and toward the idealistic future, one must set aside their will and yield. Humility opens new possibilities in life by surrendering one's wants. Once they are surrendered, grace replaces them with new wants. Grace fills the void that surrender leaves.

For James (2011, 175), humility is surrendering one's ambitions and plans. This attitude is what Augustine called being emptied. After being emptied, the subconscious power to change floods into the mind of the surrendered, giving one new energy and vitality. One is changed by an external force, as opposed to trying to change oneself. This experience is what Augustine called the Holy Spirit taking over the empty house. Humility, yielding our will, is how the house is emptied. As Jesus said before his crucifixion, "My Father, if it be possible, let this cup pass from me; nevertheless, not as I will, but as you will" (Matthew 26:39). Jesus surrendered his will, and he was filled with grace and willingly took the cross. Spectators may have seen Jesus as a prisoner, but he was free in every sense. He freely went to the cross and did so because he wanted to. When we humbly empty ourselves of our wants, we are filled with new wants.

Martin Luther (2018, 44) speaks of humility as a state of mind, one in which the person is self-deploring and despairing as a sinner. Humility realizes that salvation is out of one's reach and only given by God. Not until the sinner is brought down to "nothing" are they saved. Luther conveys the idea of emptiness. Luther (2018, 132) understood that humility prepares one for grace. He explained that the knowledge of one's sin, and the response of humility, resulted in grace.

Leszek Kolakowski (2012, loc. 628 of 4817) introduced an interesting perspective from Augustine. He explained that at times God removes the passion for godliness and doing God's will to remind Christians of their powerlessness. We are humbled by our powerlessness. Human nature has no power over sin without God's grace, and this humbling realization sparks dramatic change and renewal. Peter failed Jesus on the night before his crucifixion. Augustine believed it was because God withheld grace from Peter. Peter denied Jesus (Luke 22:54-62). After Christ's resurrection, Peter repented of his denial and was renewed by Jesus's invitation to continue to be his follower and feed his sheep (John 21:15-19). Peter's failure (humbling) and repentance (humility) resulted in the grace needed to birth the church, lead it, and initiate Gentile evangelism (Acts 2:14-41, Acts 10). Our lack of grace and the humiliating consequences are a source of change, renewal, and empowerment.

Luther (2018, 232) believed that the Law's purpose was to provide knowledge of our sin. The law produced the feeling that something was wrong. This feeling is the dissatisfaction that William James referenced when talking about a breakpoint toward surrender. The spark of change is the moment of brokenness when we say, "Lord, I need your help. I cannot do this.

I am far from what I should be." Jesus affirmed the need for brokenness if one wanted to experience God's Kingdom when he said, "Repent, for the kingdom of heaven is at hand" (Matthew 4:17). Knowing what we should be, or could be, and surrendering to the fact that we cannot be this by our own efforts, is the spark that starts change.

Grace Produces More Grace – The Snowball Effect

The understanding of most Christian leaders is that Christians should have norms of ethical and selfless behavior. They should be self-disciplined, temperate, just, virtuous, and loving. Virtually no Christian leader has taught that grace leads to perfection.[7] However, grace as a force motivates us to act the right way. The motivated heart is what God seeks. "For the eyes of the Lord run to and fro throughout the whole earth, to give strong support to those whose heart is blameless [perfect, complete, at peace] toward him" (2 Chronicles 16:9). The beauty of grace is how it steers us. We feel delight and freedom in righteousness. Grace produces ethical and selfless thoughts and behaviors through passion and free will. Grace gives joy and peace in righteousness. One has a passion for being ethical and selfless, and one freely acts. God sees and accepts the willing heart.

Think of this like a sailing ship. The ship raises its sails, and the wind drags it across the waters. There is resistance from the water. The waves and rough seas slow the ship's progress. The journey is not perfect, because there are forces that push against the ship. Despite the challenges of rough seas, the wind continues to advance the ship to its destination. Paul put it this way: "If the

---

[7] A notable exception are the Pentecostal holiness movements that teach the gift of sanctification, which is understood as deliverance from sin.

Spirit of him who raised Jesus from the dead dwells in you, he who raised Christ Jesus from the dead will also give life to your mortal bodies through his Spirit who dwells in you" (Romans 8:11). Paul then explains that as a result, we do not live according to the flesh. The Spirit has defeated the works of the flesh (Romans 8:12-13). In other words, the wind overpowers the rough seas, although we are battered as we go. Grace does not produce perfection, but it does produce change.

The Roman Catholics criticized Luther's idea that salvation was only by faith. They pointed out that salvation without works was not salvation. Keep in mind that the Catholic Church during the Reformation did not accurately portray what Luther was saying. However, the Catholic criticism did expose the danger of seeing grace as acceptance by God and nothing else. The Epistle of James explains that faith and works go together (James 2:14). This verse is consistent with the Catholic understanding that works and faith are linked. Interestingly, Luther questioned the legitimacy of the book of James and believed that it should not be in the Bible. Luther believed James wrongly emphasized works as an important component of salvation (Pohle 1909a, n. The "sola fides" doctrine of the Protestants). Luther and his fellow Protestants were then challenged to explain how good works were important to the Christian's life.

Protestants do emphasize works as part of salvation. The German theologian Dietrich Bonhoeffer states the Protestant view that grace without works is "cheap grace." "The grace which amounts to the justification of sin without the justification of the repentant sinner who departs from sin and from whom sin departs" (Bonhoeffer 1995, 43). Despite the criticisms between Protestant and Catholic theologians, often exaggerated, both Roman Catholics and Protestants express that Christians are expected to live by standards defined by the Bible.

Typically, evangelical Christians understand faith in God as having two directions. Faith has a vertical direction that looks toward God, and it has a horizontal direction that looks to those around us. Grace impacts both our love for God and our love for others. Being a Christian is understood to take place on these two planes. The first plane, the one that starts our faith journey, is a right relationship with God. This aspect of faith has to do with recognizing God's Son, Jesus Christ, as Lord. The first act of grace is that the Spirit fills one's heart with a passion for worshiping and praising God. Christians proclaim their God as worthy to be praised by all of creation.

The second, horizontal plane of faith is living in right relationship with each other. The laws of the Old Testament and the concepts of the New Testament were not designed to be rules of right and wrong; they were intended to be rules of community. As one follows the dictates of the Bible, one builds communion with others. These virtuous acts and appropriate attitudes result in a loving community. Augustine (2014, bk. 15, ch. 18) explained that all of these good works have one foundation, and that foundation is love. The Trinity is a fellowship of love. And by the Holy Spirit in the heart of the Christian, we are inspired to replicate that fellowship. This fellowship is God's love, shared with God's disciples to be imitated and shared with each other.

Augustine and Aquinas believed that grace produced works. Where there were no works, there was no faith (Augustine 2014, bk. XV, 18). Aquinas (1991, ch. 9, 114:5) explained that grace produced works that produced more grace and more works. He believed that grace first moved one to salvation, and then grace continued to move one toward a transformed life. Each desire that grace produced, once acted upon, produced more desires to do more things. Grace had this snowball effect. It inspired actions that, when conducted, inspired more actions. Karl Barth, a renowned Swiss Protestant theologian, explained that salvation is not an end to itself; it has a purpose. God's purpose is to create a community (Barth and Johnson 2019, 265). Grace moves Christians toward healthy relatedness. Our relatedness with others allows us the opportunity to express sacrificial love (an act of humility), which brings more grace.

We are going to look at two interesting views by Aquinas and Bonhoeffer on monastic life. By combining the ideas of Aquinas and Bonhoeffer, we gain a greater understanding about grace and its effect. As these theologians demonstrate, grace is the wind that pushes the ship on an amazing voyage.

Aquinas believed that the grace snowball ultimately led to a monastic life of celibacy, poverty, and obedience (Healy 2014). This level of selflessness resulted from grace moving a person to this ultimate human experience of grace, which was happiness in hardship, worship, prayer and simple obedience. Keep in mind that Aquinas' idea is that one is disposed or inclined by grace to live the monastic life. The rigors of monasticism, for the grace-filled, were delightful.

Bonhoeffer (1995, 48–49) notes that Luther was a devoted monk. In theory, Luther had reached Aquinas's epitome of grace. However, explained Bonhoeffer, grace pulled Luther out of the monastic life. Grace brought Luther out of isolation and into the "world" to perform his good works. This understanding, said Bonhoeffer, was Luther's call to discipleship. The implication was that discipleship was not an activity one conducted in isolation as a monk. Luther's ministry was too small for a cloistered monk. Bonhoeffer explained that Luther's call to ministry was more significant in the world than in the monastery. His ministry evidenced grace, more so than anything Luther had experienced in the monastery.

When Luther talked about grace, he implied it had cost him his life. What he meant was this God-given passion had brought him to the place of sacrifice. Luther's sacrifice, which he performed willingly, was to leave the monastery. Bonhoeffer (1995, 50) explained that the grace Luther experienced, demonstrated by his selfless works, was so pervasive and heartfelt that Luther overlooked the works of grace. In other words, the works Luther renounced as being in vain, he willingly did. Grace moved Luther into the monastic life of discipline and austerity, and grace moved him out of the monastic life to lead a revolution. Grace produced extraordinary works in the life of Luther.

Grace is that wind that moves the ship faster and further as one opens more sails. The key is to open as many sails as one can. How God can use us depends on grace and catching the wind.

Luther spoke of grace as being through faith and only faith. He taught that works were of minimal use for the Christian. As noted above, the Roman Catholic Church objected to the separation of works from faith. But Luther's life demonstrated that he had freely and willingly left all to follow Christ. This dynamic is what Bonhoeffer was explaining. Luther's life was full of good works. Luther's willingness to sacrifice was evidence that faith and grace had produced works. In other words, Aquinas and Bonhoeffer were both right: it was grace that brought Luther to the monastery, and it was grace that moved him out of the monastery and into a renewal movement. Grace produces works so efficiently that they do not feel like works.

The bottom line is this: the more one dances, the more one wants to dance. And dancing will take one places one never imagined he or she would go—places one once said he or she would never go. The amazing thing about grace is that sacrifice, selflessness, new behaviors, and new directions in life are all driven by enthusiasm and the persistent feeling that one is freely making their own decisions. Grace is like a snowball: the more one responds to the passion for godliness and service, the more the desire grows and moves one deeper and deeper into living their faith by selfless actions and activities. The more the ship catches the wind, the more we want to raise more sails and journey to remarkable places.

As noted earlier, the theologian Karl Rahner (1961, I:299) explained that grace divinizes Christians. From his perspective, this was not solely a statement of identity that Christians are children of God. Being divinized, for Rahner and others, was how faith functioned. Rahner saw what God did as a verb, "to divinize." Divinizing was how grace worked; it was setting the sails to catch even more wind. As Roger Haight (1979, 147) explained, divinizing is the action of participating in God's life.

A Christian that is experiencing grace is changing into the image of Christ. Each step upward to that ideal leads to more grace. Grace is like the conditioning an athlete does to become an Olympic champion. The more they work out, the stronger they get. The stronger they get, the more they want to work out. The process of grace, which leads to more grace, is the divinizing process or the snowball effect.

The following aspects of faith speak to the snowball effect of grace. Meekness, servanthood, compassion, and love are produced by grace and lead to greater grace.

Meekness

In the seventeenth century, the English minister Matthew Henry (1822, 17), in a short book about meekness, explained that meekness was what one did when domesticating wild animals. The farmer tames the horse, and it turns from wild to meek. Henry's idea was that meekness took the fight out of the wild animal. The meek are compatible and harmonious with others. The opposite of meekness is not pride; it is anger, resentment, and conflict. Anger, resentment, and conflict appear when one is not meek. The meek horse is in harmony with the farmer and other animals, and the opposite is the aggressive, wild horse. The meek are humble. But meekness is not humility.

The word *meek* in the Bible is often translated as "humble," "gentle," or "lowly." When Jesus arrived in Jerusalem on a donkey (celebrated on Palm Sunday), the English translations of the Bible say different things. The *English Standard Version* says he was "humble." *The New International Version* and *The American Standard Version* say he was "gentle." And the *New King James Version* says he was "lowly." *The King James Version* uses the word *meek*. In fact, in Matthew 21:5, the word used to describe Jesus entering Jerusalem on a donkey is the same word found in the Beatitudes: "Blessed are the meek" (Matthew 5:5). The words *meek* and *humble* are often interchanged in English, leaving the impression they are the same thing. But they are not.

The New Testament Greek word comes from the Old Testament Hebrew word *anav* (עָנָו). Jesus challenged his audience to take his yoke, to learn how to be meek, and they would find rest (Matthew 11:29). This word is used in Psalms 37:11, in a statement similar to the Beatitude of Matthew 5:5 about meekness: "But the meek shall inherit the land and shall delight themselves in abundant peace" (Psalm 37:11). Therefore, one can conclude that meekness leads to peace and emotional rest.

So how does meekness work? How does one use meekness to find peace? How does meekness help us change? The Hebrew word *anav* is based on the idea of a servant. It is related to status and ownership, and a servant has neither. A servant may be a manager of the master's possessions, but the servant does not own the possessions. The "meek" person has no status or property that they can claim for himself or herself (Friedrich and Kittel 1968, VI:647). Jesus, who was God, rode into Jerusalem on a donkey, not a horse or a chariot. Jesus came as a servant. He had surrendered his status as Lord and King of Kings. Jesus surrendered his wealth. The Creator of all creation did not reveal his possessions and did not assume his position. Jesus gave them up. Paul explained Jesus's humility in Philippians 2. Jesus was God but renounced his position as God: "But emptied himself, by taking the form of a servant" (Philippians 2:7). Paul continued by explaining that Jesus became obedient to death.

The meek are quiet; they are gentle because they no longer feel the need to defend their position or possessions. A servant knows he or she is a servant, and the servant has nothing. As a result, they are free from the stress of status and possessions. The meek are not angry or resentful. They are at rest, at peace. The servant may be a defender of their master's reputation and possessions, but the servant is not the master. The servant is not provoked by loss or insult, they have no position to defend, and they have no possessions to lose. There is no animosity against God or others when social status is challenged or when possessions are lost.

The remarkable exchange between Jesus and Pilate illustrates well that Jesus had no interest in defending his position. He was meek, a servant without position or possessions. Pilate was perplexed, and he tried to coach Jesus into defending himself. Pilate offered Jesus a way to avoid crucifixion. Pilate's strategy was to impose a flogging, which he hoped would appease the religious rulers. Pilate needed Jesus to defend himself. To Pilate's amazement, Jesus did not defend himself. When asked if he claimed to be the King of the Jews, Jesus was silent (John 19:1-16).

As Paul later explained in Philippians, God exalts the meek. "Therefore God has highly exalted him and bestowed on him the name that is above every name" (Philippians 2:9). The owner defends his faithful servants and acknowledges their importance. For that reason, the servant can quietly wait until they are acknowledged by their master.

Aquinas hinted at this idea when he said that grace, when in full effect, takes one to self-imposed poverty, chastity, and obedience. The grace-filled person willingly surrenders their status and positions. Protestants would agree that surrender is important to the Christian life, but living a monastic life is not the only way to live a meek and surrendered life. That said, meekness is a form of surrender.

"Blessed are the meek, for they shall inherit the earth" (Matthew 5:5). The owner, the master, gives the faithful servants positions and possessions. But they are not owned by the servant; the servant is a guardian, a steward. The meek only have status and resources because of their relationship to the master. The master bestows prestige and allows the use of the master's property. It is like being the chief executive officer (CEO) in a wealthy owner's company. The CEO's relationship with the company's owner results in a position in the company and access to the company's possessions. The CEO has a position and access to the company's wealth. Only a foolish CEO thinks he or she owns their position or the company's wealth. As a result of being a trusted employee, the CEO has access to the owner's wealth. The wealth is for the benefit of the owner.

Another example is the relationship between a wealthy father and his children. What is better than owning a luxurious boat and a beautiful lake house? What is better is a father who has a nice boat and lake house. The children can enjoy the wealth without the worries of ownership. If the boat sinks or the house burns, there is no cause for anger or resentment. The son or daughter is not the owner. The child benefits from the father's wealth, but the possessions are the father's concern.

How often have you felt anger and bitterness because someone violated your rights? *You have no right to talk to me that way. You had no right to take that from me. Because of my position, you must treat me this way.* Personal rights, a major source of anger and resentment, are revolutionized because of meekness. The meek do not own anything or have any prestige. The meek have surrendered their rights and, consequently, the starting point for anger and resentment. As Jesus put it, "If anyone would come after me, let him deny himself and take up his cross and follow me. For whoever would save his life will lose it, but whoever loses his life for my sake will find it" (Matthew 16:24-25). The follower of Christ claims no right to honor or ownership. The meek surrender their rights to God, and it is God who must establish and defend their rights. We are who God proclaims us to be. We only have what God has entrusted to us; we are trustees. And it is God who defends what God declares and what God owns.

Moses was called meek (Numbers 12:3). At this point in the Biblical narrative, he no longer had status in Egypt, and he had no possessions, at least not like he once had in Egypt. Moses was a nomadic shepherd. When the Egyptians and the Jews challenged Moses's position, he waited on God to defend his position. Moses understood he was God's servant and only in the position of liberator of the Jews because God put him in that position. Moses was a steward of what God allowed him to be and use. This understanding freed Moses to relax and live in peace as a leader of a nation. Moses was a servant fulfilling his master's will, and his position was solely dependent on his master. Moses got in trouble with God when he set meekness aside and took ownership of his position. When Moses took control from God, he was punished and not allowed to enter the promised land (Numbers 20:8-12). The meek surrender who they are and what they have to God. Then they trust God to defend who God says they are and preserve what God assigns to them.

As Aquinas explained, grace produces more grace. The surrender of positions and possessions, motivated by grace, produces even more motivation to surrender our positions and possessions. This perspective is what Jesus was driving at with those that wanted to be his disciples when he said they had to surrender all to follow him (Matthew 16:24-25; Mark 10:28). In Luke 18, the rich young ruler asks what he must do to be saved. Jesus said to sell all and follow him. In Matthew 28, Jesus talked about the last days and the judgment of humanity. He explained that judgment would be based on generosity to the marginalized. Jesus was not asking his followers to be poor; he was asking them to be meek. As both Moses and Jesus demonstrated, the meek are powerful because meekness allows God to be in control. The meek give their wealth to God and become stewards. What we have and who we are is placed in God's hands.

Meekness is a great spiritual workout that helps Christians become more like Christ. Only by surrender do we receive meekness. Our frustrations and flashes of anger reveal the un-surrendered rights we have in our lives. Surrendering our rights to God and being God's servant and steward is the answer. God promises that the meek will inherit the earth. God takes care of the meek. That does not mean the meek have no possessions or prominence; it only means they know that their possessions and status are from God and in the care of God. Meekness allows God's power to be manifested. Meekness is the snowball effect that amplifies humility to its deepest levels and changes our lives.

Rights, The Enemy of Grace

One of the ironic realities of being in a church over a long period is to see the number of people who come to Christ with enthusiasm and join the church, only for them eventually to leave the church and become inactive. Sadly, most leave mad or disillusioned. After a disappointment or insult, they leave the church and practice their faith outside a worshiping community of believers. The resentful and hurt go the opposite direction grace was designed to take them: they go into isolation and away from meaningful community. Bitterness always takes one out of the community and into isolation. We become bitter when somebody does not meet our expectations. We thought we had a right to something, and that right was not respected. Nothing diminishes grace like bitterness. The passion to love is replaced with the passion of resentment.

The opposite of meekness is anger and bitterness. Anger is the first red flag of danger. It indicates that a position one believes they had was disrespected or a possession one believes was theirs was taken or damaged. Our first response is anger. Bitterness is smoldering anger that continues long after the offense.

The meek do not fight for respect or possessions. They believe God will meet their needs; the meek will inherit the earth. Their inheritance is based on God's faithfulness, God's power, not by struggles with others. The meek can relax because God will defend them and provide for them. Anger and bitterness diminish the passion that God gives the believer to change and become more like Christ. Grace leads to relational reconciliation and healing. Anger and bitterness lead to broken relationships and retaliation. Anger and bitterness slow the flow of grace because they take control of our passions in negative ways.

There is an interesting story about meekness in the Old Testament. Elkanah had two wives, Hannah and Peninnah. Peninnah was able to have children. Hannah was not. The Bible says that despite not having children, Elkanah loved Hannah deeply. Hannah was broken-hearted because she was barren. She went to the priest Eli to pray and to make a vow before God. Her vow was that if she could have a child, she would give her child to the Lord. Hannah explained to Eli, who asked her why she was so upset that she felt "anxiety and vexation" (1 Samuel 1:16). The word vexation in this verse is often translated as "frustration" or causing someone "grief" or "anger." This word is used in the Old Testament to mean making someone angry.

She was angry and resentful. Her anger probably came from two sources. One obvious source was Elkanah's other wife, who could have children. Peninnah humiliated Hannah because she could not have children. Hannah would weep and become so troubled she could not eat (1 Samuel 1:6-7). Hannah's second source of anger was not as evident in the scriptures. She was frustrated with God. Maybe she blamed God. Hannah made frequent trips to the house of the Lord, trying to get God's help (1 Samuel 1:7, 9-11). And Hannah, after years of disappointment, decided to make a deal with God. She would give her first son to God (1 Samuel 1:11).

After surrendering her future child to God, her prayers were answered. She soon bore a son and named him Samuel. She then presented him to Eli to be raised in the temple. Hannah explained, "Therefore I have lent him [Samuel] to the Lord. As long as he lives, he is lent to the Lord" (1 Samuel 1:28). Hannah gave up her son. Hannah then said a prayer (1 Samuel 2) in which she affirmed that God was in control of all events, God could be trusted, and God cared for the faithful. The rest is history. Samuel became one of Israel's greatest prophets. He was the anointer, guide, and counselor to future kings and rulers.

Hannah was able to escape her bitterness through surrender. The very thing she most wanted, to have a child, she offered to God. Soon after Samuel's birth, she surrendered him to Eli, the priest, and to the temple for God's service. Her path to peace, as opposed to anger and bitterness, was found in meekness.

The meek are people who surrender their rights of ownership and status. The gift of peace from God is the consequence of surrender. Hannah was able to escape her anxiety and vexation by becoming meek. The story ends with her having five more children (1 Samuel 2:21). Hannah did not abandon Samuel. She continued to relate to him even though he lived in the temple. Her son was God's servant, and she was the caretaker of God's servant. The story of Hannah, in the Bible, concludes with Hannah's prayer. This prayer is a song of praise. She proclaims, "I rejoice in your salvation," and, "There is none holy like the Lord: for there is none besides you; there is no rock like our God. Talk no more so very proudly, let not arrogance come from your mouth" (1 Samuel 2:1-2). Hannah's song revealed that she was energized by her humility and surrender of what she valued the most.

Servanthood

Augustine believed that the natural condition of humanity was selfishness. Human selfishness, he thought, was our prison. Therefore, sin creates a whirlpool that pulls everything in life back to oneself. One's passion is for one's happiness, success, and pleasure. The selfish person can have others in their lives, but they are there to meet his or her needs. Selfishness is the state in which marriage becomes a place of self-gratification, children a source of self-glorification, and friendships a way to self-aggrandizement. As a result, believed Augustine, it was impossible for a person on their own to swim out of the "ego" whirlpool; the person was trapped by the joy of self (Haight 1979, 156).

Keep in mind that one of Augustine's main features of grace was freedom. A person is set free by grace. This freedom is so overwhelming that a person moves away from sin in ways that feel like they are making their own progress. It is like swimming out of the whirlpool, believing that your kicking is causing the progress. In fact, it is the Holy Spirit pulling you out of the whirlpool. For Pelagius, one escapes sin through their own effort. Swim harder! But for Augustine, one is freed from sin by a force pulling them.

Augustine then explained what freedom looked like. In Augustine's view, grace gives one the freedom to love (Haight 1979, 156–57), the freedom to be selfless. Grace pulls the trapped sinner out of the whirlpool of selfishness and pulls them to a place where they are free to love God and love others. "The Spirit of love is the generating force of behavior" (Haight 1979, 157). The pull of God is, in fact, a change in pleasure. The source of pleasure shifts from self to others. This change in pleasure causes the believer to fall in line with the example of the Trinity; one exists to serve others. Christ, the suffering servant, was a servant of God. As the prophet Isaiah explained, "Out of the anguish of his soul he shall see and be satisfied; by his knowledge shall the righteous one, my servant, make many to be accounted righteous, and he shall bear their iniquities" (Isaiah 53:11). Christ is God's servant and serves humanity. Thus, God is a servant of humanity, and, by servanthood, God demonstrates humility and reveals the power of grace.

Repeatedly throughout the gospels, Jesus teaches about servanthood. Paul says in Philippians 2:7 that Jesus was a servant.

In John 6:38, Jesus explains that he was sent to do God's will, not his own. Jesus told his disciples in Mark 9, when they first signed on to be his followers, that they must be servants of all. In the Passover, before his death, Jesus washed his disciples' feet and told them the road to greatness was to be a servant. During the Passover, Jesus reminded the disciples that the greater one is not the one who sits at the table but the one who serves at the table (Luke 22:27).

Augustine explained that once we are free from selfishness, we are freed to notice those around us. We see their needs, and grace impassions us to do something. When we follow the passion of grace to serve others, which is an expression of humility, grace continues to flow, inspiring us to do more. "Where there is self-transcendence, there is the movement of grace" (Haight 1979, 159). Grace takes us out of service to self, our natural tendency, and transcends us to the service of others.

In Luke 22, at the Last Supper, Jesus announces a new perspective on relationships. He explains in verse 27 that the server is greater than the served. The word used for server comes from *diakoneo* (διακονέω). This word has its origin in waiting on tables. In a more general sense, the waiter, a person who meets practical needs, is the one who is greater.

In John 13, the scriptures are more extreme. After Jesus washed his disciples' feet, he said that they should have this same servant attitude. He added that a slave (Greek – *doulos*)(δοῦλος) is not greater than the master, and a messenger is not greater than the one who sent the message (verse 16, paraphrase). Jesus concludes we must be like a slave or a messenger (verse 17). The person helping others in tangible ways is the one who is greater.

In Acts 6, the early apostles realized they needed someone to feed the hungry—in particular, to serve the tables. The people chosen for this task were called *diakonoi* (διάκονοι); later, the church called them *deacons*. Service is related to meeting tangible needs. In a more general sense, it means to edify the community through service to those in the community (Kittel and Bromiley 1964, 87). Jesus lays out his expectation for his disciples. How does one serve? As seen above, Augustine would say that through grace, one can transcend his or her selfishness and serve others. What that means is that there is joy in serving, and the more one serves, the more one wants to serve. The pleasure of serving others is freedom—that is, freedom from self.

Jesus, when peaching servanthood, was not harsh or unloving. He knew that to be great in the Kingdom of God one must be a servant. Jesus was explaining the dynamics seen in the Trinity, in Whom each serves the other. Jesus knew that the covenant of grace implants the heart of a servant into the Christian. Augustine and Aquinas explained that this is what grace does: it gives us delight in servanthood. By grace, we can serve others, and it does not feel like work. If servanthood is the way to greatness and reflects God's nature, then a hard-working servant is consistent with God's Kingdom. Communities of fellowship and communion are built on servanthood.

Servanthood produces grace, and grace is a delight in what we do for others and joy in who we are. The slave is set free by grace and is no longer a slave, but a willing and enthusiastic disciple building a community of honor and praise through service. The best dance, the one that makes everyone feel accepted and belong, is the dance of service to others. Who does not love a cheerful servant?

Compassion

Thomas Aquinas (1991, ch. 10, vol. 30) explained that distress is what a person feels when they are unable to do what they want to do. He goes on to explain that sensitivity to people in distress is one of the elements of compassion. Compassion is based on observing others who are in distress. When a person sees someone unable to fulfill their wants (distressed), the sensitive person feels compassion.

Compassion is being concerned over another person's distress. The compassionate person wants what is good for the other person. This attitude was Jesus's point in Matthew 25, where Jesus talks about the distressed, the naked, hungry, and imprisoned. He concludes that his followers should notice the distressed and serve them. "As you did it to one of the least of these my brothers, you did it to me" (Matthew 25:40). Jesus challenged his followers to be sensitive, to see those around them that were in distress.

Compassion, explains Aquinas (1991, ch. 10, vols. 30–31), produces generosity. The compassionate are enthusiastic about sharing their possessions with those in distress. By doing so, they demonstrate a lack of love for things and a love for others. What makes Aquinas' insights interesting is that they are based on one's will. The compassionate person wants to help, and he or she finds pleasure in helping. The underlying force of compassion is grace, the desire to help. The servant does not help others through forced actions. The servant willingly helps. As Paul explained in 1 Corinthians 9:7, "Each one must give as he has decided in his heart, not reluctantly or under compulsion, for God loves a cheerful giver." Grace is the breeze that pushes our will to help others. It is the passion to get involved. Compassion is sensitivity to the needs of others and the ability to follow the internal desire to get involved. As Paul noted, "Blessed be the God and Father of our Lord Jesus Christ, the Father of mercies and God of all comfort, who comforts us in all our affliction, so that we may be able to comfort those who are in any affliction, with the comfort

128

with which we ourselves are comforted by God" (2 Corinthians 1:2-3).

Compassion is different than love in that it has a narrower focus. It is focused on the distress of others. It is a grace-driven virtue to help others in need. As Christians, we have compassion for others that have need, and we freely help them. Aquinas (1991, vols. 34, 32–2) says there are seven areas of human (bodily) need and seven areas of spiritual need. The seven bodily needs are: being visited, drinking, eating, clothing, paying a ransom, providing shelter, and helping bury the dead. The spiritual needs are teaching, giving advice, giving correction, comforting, forgiving, supporting, and praying. Grace inspires the followers of Christ to meet needs, not out of law and fear, but out of a willingness to help. Compassion for others is when one passionately and willfully meets the physical and spiritual needs of others who are troubled.

Love

God's love involves God's desire to do things that benefit humans. The prophet Jeremiah put it this way: "For I know the plans I have for you, declares the LORD, plans for welfare and not for evil, to give you a future and a hope" (Jeremiah 29:11). The early theologians understood love to be the result of grace. God's grace produces in the Christian love for God and others. Love is related to a person's passion for another person's wellbeing. By grace we hope and work for their welfare, success, and future. It is like the commitment a parent has for their child's success and happiness in life. Parents willingly sacrifice their wellbeing for their child's wellbeing. The most important thing is that the child has a future and hope.

Aquinas (1991, vols. 34, 23–1) notes that one can love all kinds of things. A person can love seafood or steaks, but that is a love attracted to oneself. Besides, you cannot work for the wellbeing of seafood. That is not relational love. Trinitarian love, demonstrated by the Father, Son, and Holy Spirit, is relational love. Love for a friend or family member is relational love. In the case of love, one is passionate and willful for the other's wellbeing.

Love is a passion freely expressed. Aquinas explained that love is not the Holy Spirit loving through us as if the Spirit is an alien being within using our hearts. We would then be devoid of love; it would not be we who love, but an alien in us loving through us. Love comes from grace. The Holy Spirit connects with our spirit, and we receive the ability and desire to love another. We love because God makes us able to love through grace. Thus, explained Aquinas, grace-motivated love flows from our free will. We love because the Holy Spirit touched our hearts, and our reborn hearts choose to love. "We actually will our love" (Aquinas 1991, vols. 34, 23–2).

Augustine (2007, 221) explained that love and fear both motivate actions of good behavior toward others. He explained that a slave who fears his master's beatings would work for his master's wellbeing. Fear is a force that motivates. Augustine related fear to the purpose of the law. Its purpose is to motivate good behaviors by specifying punishments, thus generating fear. But, as Augustine explained, grace is also a force that motivates. Love replaces fear: "Perfect love casts out fear" (phrase from 1 John 4:18). Love replaces fear as the motivating force to work for another's wellbeing. Love does not want to disappoint; it wants to meet others' expectations. The point is that the desire to strive for others' well-being is love. Through grace, love becomes an act of freedom. One is free to care for others, to sacrifice for others, not through fear but love.

The Many Sources of Grace

Saying that meekness, servanthood, compassion, and love are the only sources of the snowball effect of grace overlooks the many virtues that the Bible promotes. The Bible presents many virtues that flow from grace and that produce grace. In each case, they require an attitude of surrender. As we surrender, we are inspired to more virtuous actions. By living a virtuous life, we become athletes in training, and each day, we are stronger. We go from grace to greater grace. Below is a bullet list of virtues and a brief note to explain how they produce grace. By no means is this a complete list. My point is simply to illustrate that the scriptures are full of pointers about how to start a snowball of transforming grace.

- Confession: The Bible teaches us to confess our sins one to another (James 5:16). By admitting our mistakes to someone, we express our limitations and faults. When we confess our shortcomings to others, we express humility and a willingness to change. By acknowledging our mistakes, we are admitting that we know we are a sinner in need of grace. We need to change. God gives grace to those who admit their weaknesses and mistakes, making them able to change.
- Hospitality: When we care for others by bringing them into our homes and waiting on them in tangible ways, we become servants. The interesting thing about hospitality is that it implies quality service to others. God gives grace to those who feed, entertain, and serve guests.

- Kindness: When we treat people with respect, we show more than respect; we show kindness. Kindness has to do with being cheerful and caring. A kind person speaks with affirming and encouraging words. It takes humility to be kind. A kind person applies the Golden Rule and treats others the way they would want to be treated. God gives grace to those who are positive and caring.
- Cheerfulness: Life is hard for everyone. The cheerful are not people who have no pain in life. They are people who put others first by reassuring them. The cheerful set aside their pains and think of others. They provide an atmosphere of hope. The cheerful person speaks words of hope, even during hard times. God gives grace to those who consider what others need and say encouraging words.
- Initiative: It is easy to be lazy and see things that need to be done and expect someone else to do them. Those with initiative are meek, and they do not assume they are too important to do the jobs others do not want to do. God gives grace to those who jump in and work, doing the tasks others feel are unworthy of their status.
- Generosity: Most of us expect that the future will bring hard times, and we need to save what we have. The generous are those who give instead of building bigger storerooms. They ask the question, "Can my gift make a person's life better?" The generous person shifts the focus from what is good for me to what is good for you. God gives grace to those who overcome their fears about well-being and give for the well-being of others.
- Encouragement: Human nature causes us to love talking about ourselves. Encouragement builds up another person

by talking about their positive qualities. It points out their skills and gives hope for their future success. God gives grace to those who praise others by telling them why they are of value.

- Patience: We tend to value our time more than anyone else's time. Patience has to do with time. When we are patient, we are showing that other people have value. What they do is important, and we can wait. God gives grace to those who will set aside their timeline and value someone else's timeline.

- Simplicity: One temptation we all have is to gather things to fill a void in our hearts. Things are like a drug that distracts us. Another reason for gathering material things is the temptation to find our worth in what we have. We often compare what we have with what others have. Humility involves finding peace and worth in who we are and not what we have. God gives grace to those who can live with the basics of life and trust God to bring them peace and reveal their worth.

- Gratitude: When someone does something beneficial for us, such as a deed or words, gratitude shows we acknowledge their act benefited our lives. Gratitude express that we need others in our lives to flourish in life. Gratitude is not a warm feeling of "thanks" for someone's contribution to our lives; it is acknowledgment to the one that helped us of their help. God gives grace to those who are humble by recognizing none of us could succeed in life without the help of others.

- Worship: When one participates in a worship service, one shifts their focus from oneself to God. Songs of praise for God, prayers of confession, scriptures that reflect the wisdom of God, and sermons preached that focus on our Lord, diminish us and maximize God. The worship experience puts God and us in perspective. God gives grace to those who worship His Son, and they leave the worship experienced energized and excited about pleasing God (grace).

As we have seen, grace inspires deeds of righteousness. Grace inspires us to a virtuous life that builds community. That said, any of the circumstances in life that could lead to one of the above virtuous responses could also be met with resentment and bitterness. The passion of grace can be replaced with the passion of bitterness. As the above list demonstrates, grace comes when we are humble. Love is expressed by virtues, which are concrete expressions of love. The more grace we receive, the more virtues we execute, which bring us even more grace. The followers of Christ are gifted grace, which motivates acts and attitudes that snowball and build community.

⌘

Our unique personality and what we do with our lives is a "call" from God. God calls us by grace to become who we are and do what we do. In the next chapter, we will look at how grace leads us to our vocation and personhood.

7. Our Calling and Gifts: My Dance

"But by the grace of God I am what I am." (Paul)

Paul said, "But by the grace of God I am what I am" (1 Corinthians 15:10). Who we are and what we do is all driven by grace. Our personhood has to do with who we are. We are each unique, and grace makes us unique. Our profession, gifts, and the direction we take in life is all the result of grace, and these define who we are. The word vocation is often associated with the idea of occupation. What is it that you do? What is your work, your profession? Gifts, in the Christian context, refer to skills we each have. What is that you do better than others? Knowing God's will is made realistic by grace. Which road should you take? How do you know what God wants you to do? If grace is God in us giving us passion to do those things that please God, then grace is how we become the unique person God wants us to be.

Our Vocation

In Christianity, the word *vocation* and the idea behind it have a long history. In Chapter 6, we talked about Aquinas's understanding that grace, when at its full expression in a person's life, leads them to a monastic life. His thought was a person could be so filled with grace that they willingly practiced the hardships of the monastic life. Early in Christianity, this level of sacrifice and self-denial was considered God's call, a vocation.

The word vocation is based on the Latin word *vocare*, "to call." Monks become monks because God called them to be monks. The monk had the grace to live a monastic life. For a long period in the Church's history, the "call" was understood to be towards a consecrated life, a life of service in the Church, such as the priesthood, the convent, or monasticism. Grace gave the passion for living a sacrificial life in service to the Church.

The Protestant Reformation brought a broader understanding to the idea of a vocation. John Calvin explained that grace equips church leaders to lead. Calvin referenced Augustine when talking about appropriate behavior, giving to the poor, and service in the church as a leader. He explained that what we do, we do by God's grace. The same grace that calls one to faith in Christ (a passion for Christ) is the same grace that leads one to their vocation (a passion for what one does with their life). Our work as church leaders is accomplished through grace. Calvin (1509, bk. 2, ch. 5, section 8) noted that Titus performed his ministry of exhortation, not simply as a volunteer acting by his power and ability; it was God who directed his heart to be an exhorter. Based on Calvin's perspective, grace produces the passion for doing what we do—or better still, for doing what God wants us to do with our lives.

The American revivalist, Billy Graham (1997, 38), tells in his autobiography about his "call" to ministry. When he finished high school, he planned to go to college and become a salesman. He was from a devoted Christian family, and he had no desire to be a pastor. He started in one Christian college, which he found frustrating, and eventually transferred to a Bible college. The school's dean needed someone to preach in a worship service in a small church, and he asked Graham to preach. Graham, with apprehension and low confidence, agreed to fill the pulpit. Other speaking opportunities followed, and soon Graham admitted he was developing a "nagging feeling" in his heart that God was calling him to preach. He admitted, at first, that he did not welcome the call.

Graham's experience reflects the nature of grace and God's call. One has no interest in a particular occupation, like being a preacher; then there is an awakening, a spark that starts to glow.

The nagging feeling turns into sleepless nights thinking about something one would never have considered—preaching, ministry, missions, or service in the church. Graham reported, "The inner, irresistible urge would not subside" (Graham 1997, 53). He said that at that moment, he surrendered his life to God to be a preacher. He had many questions and was uncertain about his future, but he wanted to be a preacher. Surrendering to God's will was accepting the desire God had placed in his heart.

Calvin was among the first theologians to dignify work. Not only are pastors called by God, but God calls everyone to their profession—that is, how they make their living (Boehestein 2014). The carpenter, teacher, civil servant, doctor, and fireman are all called by God. During much of church history, it was thought that only the clergy/priests and others who sacrificially served the church were called. Calvin believed that God called all to the work they did, which included one's profession (Bouwsma 1988, 74). This understanding became important to all Christians, regardless of their profession. The Christian can use their profession to bring light and understanding about God's Kingdom. The work each does has dignity and can be used by God.

The idea that God calls people to different professions to benefit humanity and that their career can serve as a platform to glorify God is connected to grace. If God gives the church worker the grace to be a pastor, evangelist, or missionary, God also gives grace to be a carpenter, farmer, nurse, professor, and accountant. The passion to be a particular profession is a God-given gift. Calvin believed our vocation was God-given and was for the benefit of the community. The farmer wants to feed others, the teacher wants to mentor and teach the children, the mechanic wants to fix the cars of those in the town, and the veterinarian wants to care for the beloved pets and livestock of the community. The "desire" is the call, and the "desire" is God-given. God servs the community by giving a call to people in that community.

The pastor and author Peter Scazzero represents current thought on God's call to each follower of Christ. He draws on a quote from John Chrysostom, a fifth-century bishop of Constantinople. "Find the door of your heart, you will discover it is the door of the kingdom of God" (Scazzero 2017, 56). Scazzero interprets this to mean that we each have a calling, a vision, a mission that God has placed in our hearts. This calling and vision are what make each unique. Scazzero then challenges each person to discover their personality, likes and dislikes, feelings, and thoughts. He calls this "growing in our faithfulness to our true selves" (Scazzero 2017, 56–57). This approach is consistent with looking within and listening to your passion, asking yourself, "What is it that I want to do?"

The idea of a calling today is much broader than an ecclesial (church) calling. A calling involves the passion God places in our hearts to do what we do and to be who we are.

Rainbow World is not a world of conformity. Everyone is unique, each with their own personality, unique dance style, dress, and flair. What makes Rainbow World extraordinary is that there is acceptance and belonging amid diversity. Another thing that makes Rainbow World amazing is that the variety of people and dances brings creativity and beauty. Rainbow World is dynamic; it is moving, changing, and consistently producing newness. Rainbow World is always fascinating. It can do this because each dancer is gifted their unique personhood and unique dance. This world of acceptance and belonging is formed around unique people who have their own way of expressing service, acceptance, and belonging.

Through their vocation each person is meeting the physical and psychological needs of others. God's grace is what gives each of us the passion and skills from within to meet the needs of others—that is our vocation. A bonus to our career calling is that our calling produces the income that meets our needs.

Spiritual Gifts

In addition to grace shaping our profession, it shapes our personhood, our identity—that is, what makes us stand out and unique. Personhood is defined as having unique characteristics. The word is associated with identity and personality. As the bishop of Constantinople stated, "find the door of your heart," find your passion, and you will discover who you are (personhood). We are the way we are because we want to be that way. In order to be what pleases God, our hope is in God's grace giving us the want to be who God wants us to be. God designs our unique identity for the benefit of others. Grace makes us who we are.

Before I continue talking about personhood, we should take a moment to reflect on what sin does to personhood. Not only does sin destroy relatedness with others, but it also destroys our personhood. The passion of human desire, self-centeredness, causes one to lose sight of who they are and their purpose. Self-centeredness and its resulting bitterness and resentment distort our personhood. God's grace, which seeks to make us unique and acceptable as a person, is overshadowed by human nature's passions, making us trite and unacceptable. As a result of sin, our personhood—that is, our personality and behavior—becomes offensive to others.

For many years there have been workshops, books, and articles on spiritual gifts. One school of thought in this area has explored the relationship between grace and spiritual gifts. In fact, grace gifts, or motivational gifts, are a school of thought that has been around for decades. The following draws from two sources to explain the concept. One is a discipleship program designed by Reverends Brian and Micaiah Tanck, called *OptIN©*.[8] The other is a workbook by Paul Ford (1998) called *Discovering Your Ministry Identity*. There are many books and articles that teach motivational or grace gifts.

The purveyors of motivational gifts divide spiritual gifts into three categories (sometimes more than three). 1 Corinthians 12:4-6 explains the three different categories. Verse four explains that there are a variety of gifts (*charismaton*). The root word of this term is *charis,* or "grace." In verse five, Paul says there are a variety of services (*diakonion*). And in verse six, there are a variety of activities (*energematon*). These are the three categories of spiritual gifts. In summation, there are different grace gifts, there are various ways of service, and there are different manifestations. For the sake of visualization, think of these categories like a lightbulb. The energy that runs to the lightbulb is the source of passion, the *charis*. The bulb is the receiver of the passion—the servant, or the electrical appliance that meets a need. The light that radiates is the energy or manifestation. Grace is the force behind the servant, and the actions they do are the manifestation.

The following is a breakdown of the three categories of gifts:

- The first group (or list) of gifts are the service (*diakonion*) gifts. The church lays hands on people as called by God for a particular service. These include things like apostles, prophets, teachers, and missionaries. The idea is that "God has appointed" (1 Corinthians 12:28), and the church

---

[8] OptIN© is a discipleship program that is funded by the Eli Lilly Foundation. One aspect of the program is a section in the workbook on motivational gifts. The Tancks are seminary graduates from Princeton Theological Seminary and pastors of the Scottsboro, Cumberland Presbyterian Church.

recognizes those appointed (1 Timothy 4:14). *Diakonia* means service. In the school of motivational gifts, the idea is that the church sets aside people for service by recognizing their call to that service. Often the church calls these people (service gifts) to the front of the congregation and acknowledges their role or title.

- The next group of gifts are the manifestation gifts. There are different manifestations, which Paul speaks of in 1 Corinthians 12:7-11: tongues, faith, miracles, prophecy, discerning spirits, etc. God gives manifestations of signs and wonders that people express at the moment the gift is needed. These gifts are referred to as signs and wonders.

- Next are the seven motivational gifts, the grace (*charis*) gifts. Paul Ford (1998, 6) says, "Each one of us is literally 'graced' with specific abilities called spiritual gifts." As Brian and Micaiah Tanck (2020, sec. Skills, Week Three, p. 2) explain, "The *charis*, the gift, that God gives each of us is different. And *charis* gives two things. God gifts us abilities for the building of the body. But God's *charis* also gives us motivation. By the Spirit, God gives us new desires."

Students of the concept of the motivational gift then present the seven gifts listed in Romans 12:6-8:

Having gifts that differ according to the grace given to us, let us use them: if prophecy, in proportion to our faith; if service, in our serving; the one who teaches, in his teaching; the one who exhorts, in his exhortation; the one who contributes, in generosity; the one who leads, with zeal; the one who does acts of mercy, with cheerfulness.

As the Tancks explain, our motivational gift may influence our personality, but gift and personality are not the same things. The grace gift (motivation) you have is your motor. It is how you engage the world around you. Your motivation does not define your profession, but it certainly influences how you do your work. For example, the grace gift of "teacher" does not mean this person is professionally a teacher (2020, sec. Skills, Week Three, p. 2). There is a unique and definable passion that each of these grace gifts has that is expressed in different ways and influenced by one's personality and profession.

The Seven Grace Gifts

The intent of sharing these seven motivational gifts is not to conduct a workshop on spiritual gifts. The intent is to show how grace is tangibly seen in our lives, making us who we are. The beauty of grace is that it feels natural; it is our passion, our vision, or desire. But in reality, it is not natural. Grace is God in us, inspiring us to do God's will. In the case of spiritual gifts, grace leads us through a motor in us that inspires our unique style. The following list of grace gifts and a brief explanation of each will help you identify how grace moves us to our unique dance.

> The Prophet: The prophet is the person gifted to protect the community from sin. This person is like the disciple Peter, and they are quick to speak and make things sound black and white. They will fearlessly confront sin, even exposing hidden sins. They are the fire alarm, helping the community identify danger. A prophet is verbal, quick to judge, sensitive to people that are not honest. This gift has a strong sense of right and wrong. Their motivation is to tell the truth and expose the truth so that all will know the truth. Their delight is to see people come to the truth and change.

The Merciful: The gift of being merciful involves wanting to help the afflicted, stand with the marginalized, and help those in emotional distress. The disciple John was a comfort to those who were tormented, and he was sensitive to people under emotional stress. He drew close to people under stress like Peter and even Jesus. The merciful sense genuine love. They are loyal close friends. They weep with those who weep, and rejoice with those who rejoice, and become angry when someone is mistreated. Distressed people find comfort in the presence of the merciful. The motivation of the merciful is to bring peace to the tormented. Their delight is to remove what is causing our pain.

The Administrator: The administrator is focused on the group and its goals. This gift likes to discover what the group wants to do, then set an ambitious goal with plans. The administrator then helps members of the group understand their role and achieve the goal. Nehemiah realized the Israelites desired a safe city. He announced the goal, organized the resources, assigned responsibilities, and helped the group build the walls. Administrators see the big picture. They break big projects down into smaller tasks and assign responsibilities. The administrator can endure criticism and can identify obstacles. This gift is sensitive to the good use of time. The motivation of the administrator is to meet the needs of the group.

Their delight is doing ambitious projects that bless others.

The Giver: The giver wants to share something of value with others hoping it will change their life for the better. The giver is sensitive to resources, and they understand the value of things. They understand the sentimental value, as well as gifts that require a sacrifice to make. Givers work hard and like to give to others. They are selective in their giving, hoping the gift has an impact on the receiver. This person wants to give in quiet ways. They give gifts that have an effect and that are inspirational to the receiver. Joseph saved grain and then gave it to people when they most needed it. He also secretly prepared elaborate gifts for his family, ones that changed their lives. The motivation of the giver is to use gifts to change lives for the better. Their delight is in giving something that has an impact on the receiver.

The Exhorter: The exhorter wants to encourage people to be all they can be. They want to teach, mentor, and challenge people to reach their full potential. Many pastors are exhorters; this grace gift is a perfect fit for service as a pastor. Paul wanted to lead others to full maturity in Christ. He thought suffering and hardships were of value, and they help one mature. This gift understands where people are at in their faith walk and can develop ways to help them grow in their faith. Exhorters like to lead small groups and have face-to-face discussions. This gift understands the importance of group unity when trying to help people mature and grow as a person. The motivation of the exhorter is that people grow in their faith and become mature. Their delight is in planning and leading people to realize their full potential.

The Teacher: The teacher wants to share the truth. The truth is derived from study and reflection. They are good students, they listen and when all the facts are stated, they speak. The teacher may see details that others overlook. This person is systematic and organized. Luke is the longest and most detailed Gospel of the four Gospels. The writer of Luke wrote Acts, another book that has excellent detail. The writer introduces both books as accurate accounts of the life of Jesus and the early Church (Luke 1: 1-4, Acts 1: 1-3). This gift is fervent in their study, and enjoys sharing with others what they learned. The motivation of the teacher is to share the truth that comes from study and observation. Their delight is to tell others what they have learned and see new understanding change lives.

The Servant: The servant wants to meet the practical needs of the people around them. They are active people (they work), and they are hands-on. They will sacrifice their time, resources, and well-being to help others. Where there is a need, the servant is a willing volunteer. This person enjoys the company of other people and only wants to know what they need. Martha was a busy person who tried to meet the practical needs of those around her. She wanted to serve Jesus by cooking and preparing the house during his visit. Jesus told Martha to stop and listen because he was there to serve her. Servants are humble and want to take care of the needs of others so that the ones served can do the more important things. The motivation of a servant is to meet practical and tangible needs. Their delight is to help people accomplish their goals. All they ask in return is gratitude.

(Taken from the OptIn workbook Tanck and Tanck, Brian 2020, sec. Skills)

Maybe you recognized yourself in one of these descriptions. You indeed recognized friends or family members. The emphasis of the concept of the motivational gift is that the gift one has is an expression of God's grace. This gift is a motor, a passion, the force that guides one's life. Underneath the personality, cultural norms, and profession of a person is their motor—their grace gift. There are things a person does that give them joy. The beauty of the grace gift is that we find joy in expressing our gift. The teacher loves to study and can find joy in isolation. The servant loves to pitch in and help and finds joy in working. The merciful loves to be a friend to those that others reject. They want to stand with the oppressed or show loyalty to a friend that is feeling down. The prophet is fearless in protecting others when they sense something is not right.

These gifts flow from the heart, and they are not forced. The gifted willingly and joyfully do what they do. It is almost an automatic response. For example, the administrator will determine the group's goal and devise a plan, even contingency plans, in the event that Plan A does not work. It is their nature, and they do not have to think about it much. They just know to do it. All the grace gifts are driven by passion, and the gifted find joy in what they do.

This understanding of unique gifts shows the power and beauty of diversity. The group can turn to the teacher to study the situation, knowing the teacher is wired to enjoy research and details. The group can call on the servant to take care of the hands-on needs, understanding the servant is wired to enjoy hands-on serving. The group can call on the prophet to discern if others are trying to manipulate the group, knowing the prophet is highly sensitive and wants to sound the alarm to protect the group.

It is helpful to know our gift and understand that gift in the context of other gifts. Often areas of contention are found when one person is frustrated that another person does not function or perceive the world as he or she does. Why do others not have the same passion I have? The teacher asks, "Why can't the servant sit down and study?" The prophet asks, "Why does the administrator overlook the character flaws of those they use to help build the wall?" The merciful asks, "Why does the exhorter push people until they are frustrated and resentful?" All gifts have excesses and need balance. The community, the body, helps each gift maximize the benefits and minimize the selfish use of the gift. Our passion, our grace gifts, are designed to be used in community. We find joy in expressing our gift. And we need the other gifts. We find unity when we each use our grace gift to do what God has called us to do in service to our community. In all cases, our gift is for others, not ourselves.

Grace and Discipleship

The German theologian Dietrich Bonhoeffer (1995, 259) explained that baptism starts the journey of discipleship. The Holy Spirit comes into our lives and makes our salvation visible. We change and people see us changing. Saying we are disciples with no visible change in our lives, said Bonhoeffer, is misleading (Bonhoeffer 1995, 47). Grace gives us the passion to conform to the image of Christ. Brian Tanck, the director of OptIN©, believes that most Christians have the grace driven passion to change, that is, to be more than they are. Their challenge is knowing how to change. Grace gives them a hunger for change, but often churches do not provide the tools they need to change. For example, Tanck notes that there are many Christians that know they should pray, and want to pray, but they have no idea how to pray. A sermon on the Lord's Prayer is not enough. The congregational renewal program OptIN© presents a new methodology of learning. It is grace driven, but instead of using a classroom and a lecture model of learning, OptIN© uses a trade school model of learning (Tanck, Brian 2021). If one wants to learn to pray (grace), one builds the skills they need to pray by learning fundamentals, practicing through repetition, then performing.

A trade school is where one learns to be a plumber, mechanic, electrician, refrigeration repairman, welder, and other hands-on professions. These people are technicians; they have technical skills. In a trade school one builds skills by doing. They learn fundamentals and build on those skills until they are able to do complex tasks. A plumber starts with learning how to join pipes; they end up knowing how to put in bathrooms and kitchens, installing an entire water and sewer system in a house. The learning and teaching methodology of a trade school has some theory, but the bulk of learning is by guided practice and repetition. OptIN© uses small multigenerational groups as their classroom. They encourage families to join the small group.

The assumption of OptIN© is that Christians do want to live the Christian life, thus acknowledging the motivating power of grace. Those skills are best developed by practice in a small diverse group. Without skills to connect to one's passion, he or she is frustrated and can become apathetic. Many churches have people who have been in church for years and have no skills. They cannot pray, teach, share their faith story, tell about their faith community, or explain to another person a Bible story. This is a case of having passion and no discipleship. Eventually one becomes content to sit and listen. They have the desire to be in church but few skills to do anything more.

OptIN© (Tanck, Brian 2021) uses dancing, in particular ballet, to illustrate their methodology for learning new skills. The ballerina starts their day at the barre. The barre is a long banister in front of a mirror. The dancer stretches and goes over the fundamentals under the watchful eye of their coach. This is not a performance; it is preparation by repetition and building strength. The ballerina then goes to the middle of the room and works on their dance; this is the center workspace. The dancer uses the barre skills and connects the fundamentals into a series of moves forming a dance. The ballerina dances in front of the mirror and under the guidance of a coach. The last step is stage work. The dancer goes onto the stage prepared to dance an entire dance with costumes. The rehearsed elements of the dance are put together and are the performance. The conclusion of the stage work is a performance in front of an audience.

For example, what if we learned to pray using the steps of a ballerina? First, we need to practice the fundamentals of whatever prayer skill we are trying to develop. Let us say we want to teach public praying. The fundamentals are speaking, speaking to a group, having an outline of what to say, and as an added challenge, speaking spontaneously. The barre work would be like this: *"John, will you stand up and tell us about your father or mother in three minutes. Tell us what he/she did, what you are thankful for because of him/her, what needs he/she met in your life, and what you wish you had done better as his/her son/daughter. I will give you three minutes to think about it, then stand up and tell us about your parent. John, just say what comes to your mind."* John has an outline, and he is going to talk publicly and spontaneously about one of his parents.

The next step is center work. Center work might look like this: a coach might lead John through a series of questions related to prayer. Who are you praying to? What are you thankful for? What are mistakes we make that cause us to feel bad? What do we need? After the questions the coach then puts John on the stage and asks him to put those answers into a prayer and pray before a small group. The coach is by his side, helping him if he falters in his performance.

OptIN© starts with the assumption that God gives grace to the heart of the believer, and they desire to perform. What is missing are the skills. The OptIN© approach looks at all Christian disciplines as skills that can be learned through a progression that starts with fundamentals and culminates with performance.

A big key to learning new skills involves failing. Each person who wants to learn new skills must understand that taking risk and failing is how one learns in trade school. There is always a pile of mistakes in the corner. Our first efforts lead to rustic and modest results. We set goals, we practice skills, and we fail and learn. If we all understand that failing is acceptable and even encouraged, then we will learn new skills. Risk taking is celebrated because it leads to humility and produces God's grace, which impassions us.

Grace is the energy we need to pursue discipleship. We need a mentor, a coach, and grace to learn new behaviors and new skills. It is easy to learn when one is enthusiastic. Grace brings the enthusiasm. God's Kingdom is relational; we learn through relationships. Christian leaders introduce us to the skills we need. OptIN© illustrates a way this can happen. We can learn skills by building from the fundamentals to performance.

The question for Christian leaders is what are the skills Christians need? In the case of OptIN©, the program identifies five categories of skills: being a follower of Christ, prayer, telling our faith story, serving our church, and being good neighbors. OptIN© believes it is grace that gives Christians the willingness to develop skills and the energy to implement those skills. The interesting aspect of OptIN© is it starts with a theology of grace as described in this book, and it builds Christian skills around that theology (Tanck and Tanck, Brian 2020, sec. Skills).[9]

Grace and God's Will for Our Lives

If grace can guide us into our vocation, help us express our spiritual gifts, and inspire us to learn skills, can grace also guide us in making decisions? The Wycliffe Bible Translators website guides Christians in discerning God's will. Wycliffe is a specialized mission organization that trains and deploys Bible translators around the world. Consistent with many other books, blogs, and articles on discerning God's will, the Wycliffe website lays out a multi-step process to discover God's will. The web article highlights seven principles for discerning God's will, and they are the following:

---

[9] The OptIN© concepts were taken from an OptIN conference (Tanck and Tanck, Brian 2020) and the OptIN manual.

dive into the Bible, surrender your own will, pray, look at your circumstances, ask advice, ask God for wisdom, and then act (Paredes 2015).

Most guidance on determining God's will falls along these Wycliffe lines. These are sound principles. However, when the question is asked, Should I take this job? Or should I be a missionary in this country or that country? Or should I marry this person? Or should I buy this house? It may be these principles fall short. The Wycliffe article concludes by telling the person seeking God's will to do God's will. In a way, the seven tips end where they start. How do we know God's will for what we should do? Answer: Just do God's will. The principles are not specific enough to give precise direction. Other than a clear verse from the Bible, a voice from heaven, or a clear command from someone we talk to about what we should do, none of the tips are terribly specific. They are not wrong; they just do not go far enough.

The dilemma of knowing God's will leads us to grace. After the above steps are taken, there is one more, and it may be the easiest step. What do you want to do? What if God gives you the want, the desire, to do what God wants? Grace is a vibrant force from God's Spirit that impacts all parts of our life. Just like gravity holds us to the earth, and makes water fall from the pitcher into our glass, so too, grace is everywhere and always working. It is so "everywhere" we overlook it. But when we need it, grace is there to save, sanctify, equip for service, and give us God's direction.

There are times we just do not know what we want to do. We know the options before us, but we have no clear desire for one option or the other. In that case, more than praying for wisdom, we need to pray for grace. God give me the grace to know what I should do. Paul ends all of his letters saying, "Grace be with you". Unfortunately, many interpret that statement to mean "love." It clearly is not love. Paul is not stylistically ending his letters saying,

"Love, Paul." In 2 Corinthians 13:14, Paul says, "The grace of our Lord Jesus Christ and the love of God and the fellowship of the Holy Spirit be with you all." These are three different things: grace, love, and fellowship. Only a few of Paul's letters end talking about love. Yet all end by wishing grace. Paul is frequently calling on grace to lead the believers in these different cities and churches.

When talking about his call to be an apostle and the work he performed, which included suffering hardships, Paul said, "But by the grace of God I am what I am, and his grace toward me was not in vain. On the contrary, I worked harder than any of them, though it was not I but the grace of God that is with me. Whether then it was I or they, so we preach, and so you believe" (1 Corinthians 15: 10-11). What called Paul to apostleship was grace, and what directed his ministry was also grace. He concluded all his letters with the charge that they, too, receive grace. God's grace would take them to where God wanted them to be.

There is nothing more refreshing than knowing God's will. After prayer, reading scripture, talking to trusted friends, and looking at the situations, we know what God wants us to do if there is a strong feeling to do something. When God gives us the "want," we follow it. What do you want to do?

The Problem of Pride and Knowing God's Will

Someone is already asking, "Should we follow all our desires? Should we just do whatever we want to do all the time?" The answer is yes and no. Theologians like Augustine, Aquinas, Calvin, Luther, and others all warn of following our human desires. The question then becomes how one separates their carnal desires from God's grace. Grace moves one toward God's will and human desires to self-centeredness. How do we follow the passion of grace and not the passions of lust, avarice, envy, gluttony, or greed? They are all desires. Following the right desires is complicated because grace is so embedded in our hearts that it feels like our will, passion, or desire. How does one know that their passion is grace and not just their own human and selfish desires?

Aquinas starts his discussion of human desires and grace with the problem of pride. In the Garden of Eden, there was neither pride nor selfishness. Grace was all there was. Adam and Eve moved through life, always desiring what God desired (Aquinas 1991, 403). But pride refocused Adam and Eve, and they each became the focus of their life. They were not focused on God, or even each other, but on themselves. Their desire was for themselves. The spark that started them to sin was coveting the power and wisdom of God. They wanted to be like God. They wanted to know what God knew. This desire produced pride. Adam and Eve decided their wants were more important than what God wanted (Genesis 3:5).

From Aquinas's perspective, pride is the vehicle for all of our sins, and coveting is the spark that gets pride going (Aquinas 1991, 348, 413). Aquinas drills down into pride, explaining that pride is produced from one basic desire, which is covetousness. Once pride is in bloom, it ignores God. Pride is the horse that carries all the sins on its back, but covetousness is the whip that gets the horse going. Adam and Eve coveted God's wisdom and power. Pride then moved God out of the way so that Adam and Eve could fulfill their human desires. Soon after, pride started moving everyone out of the way so that no one was in the way. Cain killed Abel because he wanted what Abel had: acceptance. As C.S. Lewis (2001, 122) explained, "Pride is the complete anti-God state of mind."

God fights sin using the same weapon sin uses. Human desires are destructive, selfish, and sinister, and they are humankind's downfall. Sin falsifies grace by giving desires that result in dishonoring God and are destructive to humanity. Grace builds relationships and community; pride destroys relationships and community. God's grace is a flood of new desires to honor God and live in right relationships with others. Grace comes from humility; sin, from pride. Grace comes from surrender; sin, from coveting. Grace produces the glorification of God and honor for others, and sin, the glorification of self. These realities give us a way to know the difference between our desires. There are only two classifications of desires: selfish and selfless. Selfishness produces conflict and separation, and selflessness produces relationships and community.

Paul points to the war within that all Christians endure. Grace goes to war against our human desires. "For I delight in the law of God, in my inner being, but I see in my members another law waging war against the law of my mind and making me captive to the law of sin that dwells in my members" (Romans 7:22-23). Aquinas explained that we do not have to be controlled by our lower nature (human desires). He pointed to Genesis 4:7, where Cain is contemplating the murder of his brother Abel. God says, "Sin is crouching at the door. Its desire is contrary to you, but you must rule over it" (Aquinas 1991, 384). We are not slaves to our lower nature; grace can rule over human desires. Cain murdered his brother, but the passion to murder was not unbeatable. Is murder selfless or selfish? As C.S. Lewis (2001, 178) explains, "The natural life in each of us is something self-centered, something that wants to be petted and admired, to take advantage of others' lives, to exploit the whole universe."

By putting the intent of grace together with the steps of knowing God's will, one can see a path to discerning God's will for specific things. Which desires are from God, and which desires are from our human nature and dangerous? There is no doubt that Cain wanted to kill Abel, so was that God's will?

Godliness is found in humility and surrender. Godliness is found in honoring God and not oneself. Godliness is expressed in serving others as opposed to selfishness. Cain was covetous. He wanted the recognition that God gave his brother. Pride always inspires us to remove those who have what we want. If we cannot be happy with what we have, why do we think we will be happy with what we covet? This understanding was Aquinas's point; coveting is the spark that detonates pride. What Cain wanted was based on jealousy of his brother. God's challenge to Cain was to take a moment and think about what you want to do and why you are doing it.

Following The Steps and Using Grace to Know What to Do

One of the safeguards of avoiding destructive human desires is using our minds. The Wycliffe website talks about the importance of understanding one's circumstances and having wisdom when making decisions (Paredes 2015). Asking others who are trusted and wise about their views is complimentary to acquiring wisdom. Augustine (2007, 82) explains that being virtuous requires one to use their mind. The mind can control the flesh.

In Genesis 4, God challenged Cain to think. It was not hard for Cain to think through the hurt and consequences that killing his brother would have. Did Cain think killing his brother was selfless and that this act would improve relationships and build community? Even the most simple-minded know the answer. Obviously, when Cain decided to kill his brother, he had to stop thinking.

Our intellect helps us avoid dangerous and self-serving desires. All humans have a mind, and most can use it to stop destructive and harmful passions. Humanity, both religious and non-religious, understand that indulging certain passions will only lead to destruction and pain. We are given a mind to look at circumstances and analyze the situation to keep us from following destructive wants. God gave us minds to reason out what we should do. In the case of Christians, not only do we have a mind, but we have the added benefit of grace. There is always a gentle nudge in our hearts when we come to a crossroads to pick the selfless path.

Another safeguard available to Christians is scripture. The Bible provides information as to what desires are harmful. The Bible talks about the desire of lust, and then it gives details as to responsible sexuality. The Bible talks about the dangers of anger, anxiety, and revenge. Many scriptures give guidance on desires related to greed and exploitation. The Bible provides concepts that help one determine what the boundaries are as far as human desires go. All of these concepts are consistent with humility, honoring God, and concern for others in the community.

Prayer is often referenced as one of the most important ways to determine God's direction. When one is trying to evaluate God's direction, the idea is to pray for a clear mental understanding that validates what to do. Some pray for a burning bush and God's voice to clearly speak God's will. But when this does not happen, what next?

Paul's letters remind us of the importance of grace. As Paul often did in his letters, he prayed that his coworkers in Christ be given grace. Our prayer is for God to give us direction through touching our hearts, by giving us a passion. "Lord, fill me with your grace." We pray that God protects us from the temptation of our human nature. The countermeasure to natural desires is grace.

Grace flowers from humility. When we pray for grace, we pray that God gives us a passion for what God wants from us.

"What should I do?" Think about your situation and circumstances. Gather the insights of others to help better understand the situation. Reflect on scripture and concepts taught in the Bible. These steps help us set fences and corral our natural desires. We profess anew our commitment to surrender to God. Then we pray for God's grace. God in us leading us requires that we then search our heart and follow the passion. Grace saves, grace sanctifies, and grace leads us. What do you want to do? There is a good chance that if you have checked all the above safeguards, your "want" is God's want.

Rainbow World is a world, not a dance hall. It is a world of streets, families, towns, businesses, schools, and communities. It is a world of relationships and making daily decisions. And it is a world whose citizens desire to dance. They have their own unique styles and qualities. Their God-given dance is a dance that produces acceptance and belonging. There is always the temptation to stop dancing and do one's own selfish things. As a result, there are moments when one must reflect on one's passions. Are those passions outside God's expectations? One must make decisions about where to go or what to do in Rainbow Word. The desire to dance, which is from God, will always reveal itself. The passion within that causes each to dance leads him or her down the roads of Rainbow World to where they need to be, dancing as they go.

8. Scriptures in the Light of Grace: The Dancers' Handbook

We are in a new covenant that empowers transformation.

The New Testament presents the idea of the covenant of grace. This covenant is a new approach to salvation. The Old Testament announced the hope of a covenant that would lead to reconciliation with God and community. The New Testament explains what the covenant of grace looks like. We will reference different verses in the Bible to see how these ideas are explained. We will look at verses that theologians cite to explain grace. Many of these verses are the better-known verses that talk about grace. These verses are a handbook on dancing.

Grace

Philippians 2:12-13 — "*Therefore, my beloved, as you have always obeyed, so now, not only as in my presence but much more in my absence, work out your own salvation with fear and trembling, for it is God who works in you, both to will and to work for his good pleasure.*"

Although the word *grace* does not appear in this verse, this text has historically been used to define grace. Protestants developed the *Westminster Confession of Faith* in the mid-1600s. It reflects the theology of the early Reformation, as well as the classical Augustinian concept of grace. When talking about grace, the *Confession* references Philippians 2:12-13, saying, "When God converts a sinner, and translates him into the state of grace, he freeth him from his natural bondage under sin and, by his grace alone, enables him freely to will and to do that which is spiritually good" (*Westminister Confession of Faith* 1647, ch. 9, sec. 4). Grace is a healing power. This verse explains that there is a healing force that changes desires and gives skills to believers and makes them able to please God. Grace is God doing two things: making us willing (desire) and able (work) to do God's good pleasure (verse 13). The previous verse (12) explains we are to recognize that grace is a dynamic flowing river that forms our salvation. Through grace, we are becoming what pleases God. Augustine (2010, ch. 32) stated, "It is certain that it is we that act when we act; but it is He who makes us act, by applying efficacious power to our will."

Hebrews 10:29 — "*How much worse punishment, do you think, will be deserved by the one who has trampled underfoot the Son of God, and has profaned the blood of the covenant by which he was sanctified, and has outraged the Spirit of grace?*"

To reject Jesus Christ is to forfeit God's grace. Simply put, grace is from the Spirit and is bound to faith in Christ. Jesus explained to his disciples in John 14 that God would send the Helper, the Spirit, and the Spirit would teach and guide (John 14:16, 26, 16:13). The grace in Jesus—and he was full of grace—was shared with the followers of Christ through the Spirit.

Through Christ, believers receive the Spirit, and the Spirit fills them with God's grace. The recipient of grace finds pleasing God pleasurable. Thus, grace transforms one by new motivations of the heart to take on God's nature. This understanding is why it is so important that the Spirit comes. The Spirit gives the follower of Christ grace.

Grace Prophesied

Deuteronomy 30:6 — *"And the Lord your God will circumcise your heart and the heart of your offspring, so that you will love the Lord your God with all your heart and with all your soul, that you may live."*

Toward the end of the Pentateuch (the first five books of the Bible), the writer explains that real circumcision is a changed heart that wants to love the Lord. After giving hundreds of God's laws for humanity to follow, the glimmer of hope is that God can change one's heart, and the new heart will govern him or her. Then, says the prophet, "you may live." John Wesley (2013, 280) stated, when talking about the circumcision of the heart, that circumcision is "a right state of soul, a mind and spirit renewed after the image of Him that created it." The Old Testament says that a new form of circumcision is coming (Jeremiah 4:3-4), and this circumcision is not an outward sign but an inward power that changes the heart. Paul references this Old Testament prophecy in his letter to the Romans. He said, "Circumcision is a matter of the heart, by the Spirit, not by the letter" (Romans 2:29). The new heart is motivated by grace to fulfill God's expectations.

Ezekiel 36:26-27 — *"And I will give you a new heart, and a new spirit I will put within you. And I will remove the heart of stone from your flesh and give you a heart of flesh. And I will put my Spirit within you, and cause you to walk in my statutes and be careful to obey my rules."*

The prophet Ezekiel told Israel that a new day would come. And when it did, they would have new hearts and a new spirit. The old heart of hardened stone would be replaced with a sensitive heart of flesh. And because of God's Spirit in their sensitive hearts, they would want to meet God's expectations.

They would walk in God's laws and obey. Augustine noted two dynamics in these verses: God gives a new heart, and God causes us to walk (makes). "He gives what He commands when He helps him to obey whom He commands" (Augustine 2010, ch. 31). Augustine continues, explaining that grace grows in the believer's heart and makes the believer able to fulfill God's statutes and rules. Grace involves a change of the will. "And thus, indeed, he receives assistance to perform what he is commanded" (2010, ch. 31).

In the New Testament, in Hebrews 8, the writer explains the new covenant in Jesus Christ. Christians refer to this new covenant as the covenant of grace. The writer references verses found in Jeremiah 31:31-24, which speak about the new covenant that God will make, which will change hearts. The covenant of grace fulfills the law in that it makes the believer willing and able to satisfy the law. Jesus explained that the law was not what the Pharisees and Sadducees proclaimed: "Then Jesus said to the crowds and to his disciples, 'The scribes and the Pharisees sit on Moses' seat, so do and observe whatever they tell you, but not the works they do. For they preach, but do not practice'" (Matthew 23:1-3). Jesus concluded his complaint against the Pharisees by saying: "The greatest among you shall be your servant. Whoever exalts himself will be humbled, and whoever humbles himself will be exalted" (Matthew 23:11-12).

Jeremiah prophesies that God's law will be put in people's hearts. The New Testament writer then declares:

Hebrews 8:10 — "*For this is the covenant that I will make with the house of Israel after those days, declares the Lord: I will put my laws into their minds, and write them on their hearts, and I will be their God, and they shall be my people.*"

Protestants, especially those in the realm of Reformed theology, talk about the covenant of grace. The idea is that followers of God are no longer under a covenant of law but under a covenant of grace. The covenant of the law defined God's expectations. It was through obligation and fear of punishment that humanity could obey and realize community. These verses show that the covenant of grace is a different way to form a community. Through a new heart, we have the ability to change. We are no longer under the law, condemned as lawbreakers. Before grace, the law was external; it was not in our hearts. The law was a matter of obligation. We are now in a new covenant that empowers transformation and the ability to live as God expects. By grace, the law is now internal. Grace changes the heart. God's expectations for how we are to live are not obligations; they are delights.

Faith and Grace

Ephesians 2:8-10 — *"For by grace you have been saved through faith. And this is not your own doing; it is the gift of God, not a result of works, so that no one may boast. For we are his workmanship, created in Christ Jesus for good works, which God prepared beforehand, that we should walk in them."*

This verse is probably the most quoted concerning salvation, faith, and grace. By grace, we are saved through faith. These two verses of Ephesians 2 do an amazing job showing the dynamics of grace with respect to salvation. Grace is the locomotive that produces our salvation, and faith is when we take a seat on the train. Through faith in Jesus Christ, we board the train. We sit in the seat of the engineer. However, it is God that takes us. The force that transforms the sinner is grace, the locomotive. Paul explains that the force is not our force. Grace takes us where God wills us to go. We can say we surrendered through faith and got on the train, but if we must boast about our changed lives, we must boast of what the locomotive is doing.

Grace is a healing and transformative power. It produces an appetite for godliness and for honoring God. No one can boast about their godly works or passion for God. It is God in us making us willing and able to do what we do. When these verses are quoted, people stop at the end of verse 9, thus missing the point. God creates us for good works, and we are empowered to do them by a gift: God's grace. "The purpose and end of conversion, regeneration, justification, and reconciliation is a dramatic transformation of good works" (G. R. Lewis and Demarest 1996, bks. 3, 164).

The reason, I suspect, that Paul reminds us that it is not our works is because it feels like our works. Our will, our wants have changed, and as a result, we delight in where we are going. The direction of the train and our passion have become one. Where God is taking us is where we want to go. It feels like we are driving the train, but as Paul reminds us, it is God. God has laid the tracks to take us where God desires, we go. God has given us delight in where we are going by filling our hearts with a passion for the things that please God. As we express godliness, we should acknowledge that it is not us but the grace of God in us that is making us who we are.

Neither Augustine nor John Calvin would fully agree with the above explanation of faith and grace. Both would agree that every good work comes from grace. However, they would not separate faith from grace. Augustine explained, "Therefore it is from Him that we have righteousness, from whom comes also faith itself" (Augustine 2010, 25). He was saying that grace is the origin of faith. In this case, even the desire to get on the train (faith) is a desire from God. The Protestant leader John Wesley would disagree, explaining that everyone has the freedom to decide if they want to get on the train (repentance and faith). For Wesley, the train is at the station, and the door is open. All the sinners must do is surrender and get on the train. Once on the train, grace takes the believer to a new life.

Titus 3:7 — *"so that being justified by his grace we might become heirs according to the hope of eternal life."*

Once we express faith and receive grace, we are empowered by grace. God in us, pulling our will toward godliness, gives us hope for eternal life. Our assurance of inheritance is because grace is pulling us. We are justified, not by perfection, but by the new passion we have to pursue God and godliness. Being on the train is our salvation, and the passion to please God assures us of our future destination.

Jesus, Full of Grace

John 1:14, 16, 17 — *"And the Word became flesh and dwelt among us, and we have seen his glory, glory as of the only Son from the Father, full of grace and truth.... For from his fullness we have all received, grace upon grace. For the law was given through Moses; grace and truth came through Jesus Christ."*

Jesus was the Word and full of passion. Augustine (2007, 266) explained that Jesus did not become flesh, but the Word became visible by being clothed in flesh. Jesus desired to fulfill God's will and honor God as a man. This desire was so pervasive that Jesus, clothed in the flesh and full of grace, was one with God. With respect to oneness, the Gospel of John explains, in chapter 17:2, that just as the Father is in Jesus, Jesus is in his disciples.

To know Jesus is to know the heart of God. Jesus is the Word, full of God's knowledge and aware of God's plan of redemption.

What Jesus was, he shared with humanity. How? Jesus was full of grace and truth. By faith in Christ and having the experience of grace, we can know the truth. Jesus's grace is given to humanity. This is what it means to have Christ in our hearts, to have a relationship. The passions of Christ are given to his disciples. These passions reveal God's nature and God's mind. Calvin observes that the Spirit of God, an unction (enthusiasm) and the source of grace, is what Christ shares with his followers. The Spirit descended on Christ at his baptism, an unction (resulting in passion). This unction given by the Spirit to Christ is shared with humanity; thus, as Calvin (1509, bks. 2, 130) explained, we see grace to grace. Jesus, full of grace, gave his followers grace.

The Spirit empowers humanity to fulfill God's will, to live like Christ, and honor God. Thus, the law given by Moses, one designed to glorify God, was revealed by the life and words of Jesus Christ. Once again, Calvin (1509, bks. 2, 130) observes that the law "serves to show more clearly how great their utility was before the advent of Christ, who, while he abolished the use, sealed their force and effect by his death." The desire and ability to fulfill Moses's law was made possible by grace. The law and grace are not two different ways to God. They are complementary to each other. The grace and truth of Jesus is the way to understand and fulfill Moses's law. However, the law is now fulfilled by a passion to please God. Through grace we no longer live under the obligation to obey every detail of Levitical law. By Christ's grace, Christians are impassioned to honor and serve God, as well as others. Thus, the intent of the law is fulfilled.

The Mighty Acts of Grace

Acts 4:33 — *"And with great power the apostles were giving their testimony to the resurrection of the Lord Jesus, and great grace was upon them all."*
Acts 6:8 — *"And Stephen, full of grace and power, was doing great wonders and signs among the people."*
Acts 14:26 — *"and from there they sailed to Antioch, where they had been commended to the grace of God for the work that they had fulfilled."*

Grace gives Christians the want and the ability to do God's will. The signs and wonders seen in the lives of the apostles were the result of God's grace. The passion for preaching Christ, knowing that those listening were angry, was the power of grace in the life of Stephen. Even martyrs, expressing God's love, are willing to die for others. Augustine (2010, ch. 33) attributed this level of sacrifice to God's grace. Stephen preached because of grace; so powerful was its effect that his passion for the gospel superseded his love for his safety.

When the apostles laid hands on the sick, they were motivated from a desire within their hearts that moved them to act. God inspired their actions, and God manifested God's power. When the apostles went to new towns and lands, it was grace that moved them. They followed grace, and grace led them out of their churches and into cities where there were no Christians. Paul explains in Romans 15:20 that he was eager to preach the gospel in places no one else had preached. However, in Ephesians 2, Paul clearly explains that it was not him, but God's eagerness he was experiencing as if it were his eagerness. Grace led Christians to new lands and equipped them with the skills they needed to reveal God's love and power.

Grace and Humility

2 Corinthians 12:9 — "*But he said to me, 'My grace is sufficient for you, for my power is made perfect in weakness.' Therefore I will boast all the more gladly of my weaknesses, so that the power of Christ may rest upon me.*"

James 4:5-6 — "*Or do you suppose it is to no purpose that the Scripture says, 'He yearns jealously over the spirit that he has made to dwell in us'? But he gives more grace. Therefore it says, 'God opposes the proud but gives grace to the humble.'*"

In the above verses, Paul referenced his thorn in the flesh. He stated that his thorn was given to him by Satan. But what Satan intended for harm became a benefit. First, said Paul, the thorn kept him "from becoming conceited." Second, as the verse above reveals, it became a source of grace and power. His thorn in the flesh humbled Paul, and this challenge produced more passion for God and more remarkable manifestations from God.

James explains that God put his Spirit into the hearts of men and women. God, through God's Spirit, gives grace. And the door one must open to receive God's grace is humility. James concludes his declaration about grace by challenging those around him to "submit" to God. If one wants their will to bend toward God's will, they must surrender, which is an act of humility.

Calvin (1509, bk. 2, ch. 2, sec 11) stated that the first principle of faith is humility. Then he added that the second and third principles of faith were also humility. We only stand by God's mercy and grace, not by anything we do. What we are is forgiven, an expression of God's mercy. What we become is holy, an expression of God's grace. As the Pharisees demonstrated, their passion was to proclaim their piety and gain the glorification of others (see Matthew 23). One knows they are self-glorifying when they applaud their own piety and accomplishments. Thus, pride shuts the door to grace.

The prideful are left with what they have, which is very little. Humility opens the door to God's grace, giving us more than we ever had or ever could imagine. Through humility our will runs toward God, and we are infused with new God-given abilities to fulfill God's call on our life. As Paul determined, by hardships, humility, and grace, the transformative power of God rested upon him.

Grace and Righteousness

Romans 5:17-21 — *"For if, because of one man's trespass, death reigned through that one man, much more will those who receive the abundance of grace and the free gift of righteousness reign in life through the one man Jesus Christ. Therefore, as one trespass led to condemnation for all men, so one act of righteousness leads to justification and life for all men. For as by the one man's disobedience the many were made sinners, so by the one man's obedience the many will be made righteous. Now the law came in to increase the trespass, but where sin increased, grace abounded all the more, so that, as sin reigned in death, grace also might reign through righteousness leading to eternal life through Jesus Christ our Lord."*

John Calvin, referencing Augustine, explained that the law (God's expectations for humanity) informed humanity of its guilt. The law and the resulting guilt revealed God's intent. If God intended to destroy the sinner, there would be no consciousness of guilt—just destruction. The law increased the sting of sin. The law defined and characterized sin, producing guilt. The law did not create sin. It revealed it like a light illuminating an infestation of rats. God intends to transform the repentant sinner by first revealing their sins. But God does not stop with the law and revealing sin; God intends to transform the sinner. Calvin (1509, bk. 2, ch. 7, sec. 7) explained that this is where grace enters. If there were no grace, then all that is needed is for the law to convict and slay. The guilt we feel defines what needs to change. Grace is the solution to God's expectations, and the law reveals those expectations, and grace comes to our aid, granted by God's mercy.

Romans 1:5-6 — "*Through whom we have received grace and apostleship to bring about the obedience of faith for the sake of his name among all the nations, including you who are called to belong to Jesus Christ.*"

Calvin (1509, bk. 2, ch. 3, sec. 13), quoting Augustine, explained that obedience to God was the consequence of grace: "The Lord draws men by their own wills; wills, however, which he himself has produced." Calvin (1509, bk. 2, ch. 3, sec. 13) explained that grace produces in the heart the decision to do the good we do. Calvin concluded that the only way one decides to be obedient to God is by grace, which is a new will to obey that grace has produced.

Christ explains his obedience to his Father ("I do nothing on my own authority"), and then calls on his followers to be obedient ("abide in my word") (John 8:28-32). Christ's appeal is made in the context of grace. Obedience is not based on following an external and impersonal code of conduct. It is based on a law that God has put in our hearts. It is personal and it is heartfelt. Obedience is also following the call and purpose God has for our life. Obedience is no longer following external laws through forcing our wills to obey; it is following internal passions that give us pleasure.

Disobedience produces passions that lead to sin and separation from God, resulting in death. But God's grace produces obedience through passions and then deeds that evidence our desire for righteousness. The change in heart, in our appetite, leads to relational connections and to eternal life. Grace conquers sin's hold on the sinner, making the desire for godliness more potent than the desire for sin. There is a war of desires within the Christian's heart, but grace abounds. Aquinas (1991, 592) states, "More was restored to man by Christ's gift, then he had lost by Adam's sin." Finding lasting pleasure in obedience to God is far superior to living by our human and destructive passions, which give superficial and fleeting pleasure.

Romans 6:1-2 — "*What shall we say then? Are we to continue in sin that grace may abound? By no means! How can we who died to sin still live in it?*"

Perfection is not the goal; it is dominion. Does sin have authority to rule, or does grace have authority to rule? This question is related to the will, to who controls our will—that is, our desires. Obedience does not produce a sinless life; it produces a life with direction. There is an ongoing war, and battles are won, showing there is life in us. Grace ultimately has more authority than sin, and grace abounds. Sickness is greater than health, but healing is greater than sickness. Sin imprisoned humanity into selfishness, but grace heals the heart of humanity and births a new heart that desires obedience to God. Our obedience reflects selflessness and honor and praise of others. This changed heart of passion, despite our imperfect works, is the path to eternal life. Our salvation is in a new heart birthed by grace that desires to please God. Through grace, our will turns toward God. By no means do we continue in the dominion of sin. Grace is a new ruler of our will, willing us to righteousness. Our freedom in Christ is real freedom. The grace within our hearts changes our will so that it wills what God wills. What can we say then? As followers of Christ, do we continue in sin? No! Grace bends our will so that we freely and willingly seek to honor and please God.

Grace and Works

1 Corinthians 3:10 — "*According to the grace of God given to me, like a skilled master builder I laid a foundation, and someone else is building upon it. Let each one take care how he builds upon it.*"
1 Corinthians 15:10 — "*But by the grace of God I am what I am, and his grace toward me was not in vain. On the contrary, I worked harder than any of them, though it was not I, but the grace of God that is with me.*"
2 Corinthians 9:8 — "*And God is able to make all grace abound to you, so that having all sufficiency in all things at all times, you may abound in every good work.*"

In 1 Corinthians 3, Paul presents the idea of laboring together. He explains that God gave him grace, and as a result of God's grace, he (Paul) built a strong foundation. Then he describes how others joined the effort, and they built upon what Paul had done. Each person played their role in God's work. Each person is inspired by grace to do what they do, and each person's labor builds on what God is building. God is building a Kingdom that transcends all other Kingdoms.

Calvin noted that grace was why Paul labored for Christ. Drawing on Augustine to amplify his idea, Calvin (1509, bk. 2, ch. 3, sec 13) explained that grace made the unwilling willing. And because the follower of Christ is willing what God wills, his labor is not in vain. The labor performed is the labor God desires to be done. Our labor could not be in vain because it is God's plan. The believer is willfully doing what they do. God in them provides them with the desire and ability to fulfill God's plan. God's plan is expansive, greater than anyone's generation or any one culture. By grace, each person, each generation, each culture fulfills their part.

The non-Christian often assumes that the only way Christians voluntarily give their money to the church or other Christian ministries is that they are forced. The non-believer has not experienced grace, so they can only imagine that sacrificial acts are obligated. In the non-believer's mind, giving puts the churchgoer in a painful situation; they must grudgingly give. It is hard for non-Christians to imagine a person giving away their money with the consistency of a tithe and it not be an obligation. Consistent giving for a non-believer is like making payments on a large debt or paying taxes. There is little joy in that.

Why are people who are not wealthy giving away so much of their money? It must be that they are simple minded, or they are being manipulated. Paul explained that each person who gives must do so from the heart. They should not give from compulsion but from a cheerful heart. Then Paul talks about grace in 2 Corinthians 9:8. Because grace abounds, we are always content with all we have. We give our time and resources cheerfully because we feel confident in God's care and want to give. Our good works of giving are motivated by grace. There is no greater joy in giving than when one gives with a willing and cheerful heart.

Ephesians 3:7-8 — "*Of this gospel I was made a minister according to the gift of God's grace, which was given me by the working of his power. To me, though I am the very least of all the saints, this grace was given, to preach to the Gentiles the unsearchable riches of Christ.*"

Paul fully understands the origin of his call to preach and evangelize gentiles. He can preach because God gave him the desire to preach. Grace is an expression of God's power. When grace leads us by changing our will and giving us abilities, grace then demonstrates power through us. Paul qualifies the power of grace by explaining that he was not a worthy saint. We all know Paul's past; he was a murderer of saints. Despite being last in line, as far as saintliness, grace was given to him. The passion God gave Paul was for people almost every other Christian of that day overlooked. Paul was passionate and equipped by God to reach the Gentiles. The many missionary journeys of Paul, and the many signs and wonders he performed, were the result of grace guiding and empowering him to do ministry. Paul willingly did what God wanted him to do.

2 Timothy 1:8-9 — "*who saved us and called us to a holy calling, not because of our works but because of his own purpose and grace, which he gave us in Christ Jesus before the ages began.*"

Augustine understood grace and God's calling as a joint effort. Christians are not alone in their works. They are called, which implies a partnership with God. Paul did not merit salvation, but by God's call and the grace given to Paul, Paul became a co-laborer with God (Augustine 2010, ch. 12).

God saves us and calls us to work. We are called to accomplish God's purpose through grace. In the prior verses of 2nd Timothy 1:9, Paul talks about his imprisonment and suffering. His hardships are his holy calling to suffer, even to be imprisoned. This harsh work is not drudgery for Paul—not even the suffering and imprisonment. Grace led Paul to profess his faith, preach, and suffer imprisonment.

2 Thessalonians 2:16 — "*Now may our Lord Jesus Christ himself, and God our Father, who loved us and gave us eternal comfort and good hope through grace, comfort your hearts and establish them in every good work and word.*"

Grace gives us comfort and hope. When we suffer in our labor for God, grace sustains us. Despite the suffering, we continue to "will" service to God. As Stephen illustrated ("full of grace," Acts 6:8), grace conquerors suffering, even if that suffering leads to martyrdom.

Titus 3:5-8 — "*He saved us, not because of works done by us in righteousness, but according to his own mercy, by the washing of regeneration and renewal of the Holy Spirit, whom he poured out on us richly through Jesus Christ our Savior, so that being justified by his grace we might become heirs according to the hope of eternal life. The saying is trustworthy, and I want you to insist on these things, so that those who have believed in God may be careful to devote themselves to good works. These things are excellent and profitable for people.*"

Works are part of our salvation. However, our works are not our accomplishment, and our righteousness is not because of our achievements and effort. By faith in Christ and the regeneration of the Holy Spirit, we are justified by grace. Titus 3 did not say we are justified by faith. Faith in Christ opens the door. Grace comes into our hearts and does the work of justification. Grace makes us just by changing our passions. We who have believed, by faith in Christ, can devote ourselves to good works. It is not us doing the works. It is grace inspiring us to do good works. The passion, the will to do good works, despite the imperfections of our works and our battle with human desires, results in God's acceptance. We are heirs with Jesus Christ because we have hearts willing to pursue holiness.

These verses illustrate why many Christians are confused about works and salvation. Verse 5 says that works do not save us. Then in verse 8, it says to devote yourself to good works. The understanding of grace explains the difference. Works that are from God's grace lead to justification. It only makes sense that if grace is God in us, causing our will to do God's pleasure, our works' direction is toward God. However, if what we do is not directed by grace, then we are following our human desires. Why we do what we do is important. If the "why" is God's grace in us moving us to work, then that work is not in vain; that work matters. We are doing God's work, and, because of grace, loving the work we do.

However, some people do good works with wrong motives. Their works are done to control others, gain personal benefit, and gain notoriety. Look at the story of Acts 5:1-11. Ananias and Sapphira were generous, but it was for personal gain and fame. They were confronted for their deception and fell dead as divine punishment. The passion behind our works determines the merit of our works. If the passion is from grace, our works have merit. If the passion is from human desires, always self-serving, then those works are in vain.

Human Grace – Words Matter

Ephesians 4:29 — "*Let no corrupting talk come out of your mouths, but only such as is good for building up, as fits the occasion, that it may give grace to those who hear.*"

Chapter 1 explained the origin of the word grace. Grace is based on the idea of a person responding to a special gift or act by feeling delight or favor toward the giver. Their delight is called grace. Human-generated grace is a feeling of motivation for another person's good because of what they have done. This feeling of delight was the origin of the Greek word *charis*.

Paul, in Ephesians 4, talked about anger, bitterness, slander, and malice. He warned Christians that attitudes and words were important. Christians do not want to disappoint God with corrupt words and actions. He then said to say nice things to each other, be kind, and forgive each other, because "it may give grace to those who hear." This idea takes grace back to its secular roots. There are things we can do and say that cause people to feel fondness toward us. Kindness can cause others delight. We can find favor in someone's eyes because of how we treat them. They are motivated to respond to us in positive ways because of what we say or do. They like us because they have a want in their heart to like us, one produced by something we did for them.

God's grace to us is a roaring river. God's grace can supernaturally be put in our hearts by faith in Christ. The grace we give to others—human grace—is not something we can miraculously put into someone's heart. It is also not the roaring transformative fire that God places in our hearts. However, there are things we can do that cause grace in others. By our words and actions, we can elicit human grace out of the hearts of those around us. Through generosity, hospitality, compassion, and kindness to others, a person can feel delight; they can feel favor towards us. Granted, this is human-generated grace, but as Paul explained, it can "build up" our relationships.

The Enemy of Grace

Hebrews 12:14-15 — *"Strive for peace with everyone, and for the holiness without which no one will see the Lord. See to it that no one fails to obtain the grace of God; that no 'root of bitterness' springs up and causes trouble, and by it many become defiled."*

The enemy of grace is not doubt; it is bitterness. Bitterness is like a root; it runs deep in the heart and holds fast. Bitterness involves the sleepless nights of reliving an injustice. The emotional energy of bitterness is so intense that as long as one is bitter, the effect of grace is stopped. If one is hurt and bitter about something that happened, it is hard to be moved by grace. Our bitterness imprisons grace, and one of the consequences is the inability to follow God's passion, which leads us. The passion that God puts in one's heart is buried under the weight of resentment. This resentment is one reason forgiveness is so important: it frees us from bitterness. Once free, we can feel grace (passion) moving us in the direction God wants to take us. As well, holiness (holy living) and peace are how others can see the presence of God in our lives. Thus, says the writer of Hebrews, strive for peace.

9. Conclusion: I Want to ~~Change~~ Dance

Physicists often speculate about what existed before the Big Bang, and what happened immediately after the Big Bang. In the same way, theologians speculate about God before creation and humanities' behavior and freedom in the Garden of Eden. Before creation, God was full of grace. Grace, a gift from God, was then given to the newly created. Once sin entered creation, God remained consistent: grace was the solution. Thanks to Augustine, we have a better understanding of how grace can be a force of change. We are not powerless or hopeless in our sins. By grace, we who could not dance can dance.

Grace, a Force from Creation

Rainbow World existed before there were rainbows. The Garden of Eden was the perfect world. Adam and Eve danced. They danced with God. They were full of grace. As the result of God's grace in them, which is the very nature of God, they lived in a perfect community. God had created a community in the image of God (Genesis 1:26-27). God, a community of the Father, Son, and Spirit, fully in love with each other, made the Garden of Eden in God's image. God danced, and God's creation danced. Adam and Eve accepted and honored each other. They had no shame, they shamed no one, and they enjoyed creation together. They had communion. Adam and Eve lived this way because they wanted and willed to live this way. They were full of grace, and their desires ran toward God and each other. They followed their will, and they were free. In the Garden of Eden, their will and God's will were the same. They freely and joyfully loved and pleased God—they danced.

Sin came from temptation. It was not Eve or Adam's idea to disobey God. But it was their decision to do so. Satan explained to them that they could have more than they had. Adam and Eve coveted; they wanted to know what God knows. They became dissatisfied with who they were and wanted more. To do this, they had to move God out of the way. They disobeyed God, doing the one thing God asked them not to do. Pride gave them the confidence to do what was pleasing to them. Human desires were born, and the grace they had lived by was vanquished. Instead of grace, they lived by their human desires. Human desires filled the void left when grace had left. They no longer wanted to dance.

The generations that followed Adam and Eve realized they were broken. The conflict and pain created by sin made sin obvious. They may not have seen it in themselves, but they certainly saw sin in others. We are all righteous in our own eyes. The consequence of sin is the tendency to relate to others with self-serving motives, resulting in dishonesty, manipulation, conflict, bitterness, and separation. Humanities' relationship with God was broken, and the brokenness extended to everyone around. Brokenness was expressed as conflict, unfaithfulness, abuse, war, anger, and cruelty. As a consequence of sin, there was pain and suffering.

Sadly, selfishness is an obsessive, singular focus, and it is a desire for self and self-gratification. All others in our life become tools for our self-fulfillment. Because of self-centeredness, we never find lasting fulfillment. We experience fears, conflicts, and isolation. Sadly, selfishness holds us prisoner. Our human desires imprison us and isolate us. No one likes to suffer, and when we suffer in loneliness, it hurts even more.

Adam and Eve built our prison, which was this: *we* want what *we* want. "Wretched man that I am! Who will deliver me from this body of death?" (Romans 7:24). How can we change? How can we escape our prison and dance again? How can we find acceptance, belonging, freedom, and joy?

Sin had so destroyed humanity that God sent God's law into the world to explain what "rightness" and "righteousness" looked like. Human desires had taken humanity far away from righteousness. Humanity had little idea what right living involved. Sin took humanity to the threshold of annihilation (see Genesis 6). Humanity needed a guide to define righteousness. God, through Abraham, the Israelites, and Moses, showed humanity what rightness looked like. Paul explained, "...Since through the law comes knowledge of sin" (Romans 3:20). Paul later said, "Yet if it had not been for the law, I would not have known sin. For I would not have known what it is to covet if the law had not said, 'You shall not covet'" (Romans 7:7). The law was not enough. A video on what dancing looked like was not dancing. And knowing what dancing looked like did not mean one wanted to dance. "I see in my members another law waging war against the law of my mind and making me captive to the law of sin that dwells in my members" (Romans 7:23). Despite having the law to guide us about right living, we were not free. We were slaves to selfishness. Would we ever be free to dance?

For change to be real, a person's will has to be changed. If the will is not changed, a person may still do "right" things, but they revert to their old nature as soon as they are free from the obligation. The lack of will to change was the shortcoming of the Old Testament law. One can legalize righteousness and force rightness, but it is inadequate. The law has to be enforced on an unwilling heart. Obligation was the best the law could do; rightness was compulsory. The law set boundaries and punishment. If you did not dance, you were punished. The result was that one danced and hated dancing. When one finds no pleasure in dancing, they will stop. This approach was no way to live and flourish in life.

The solution was to be happy in holiness. One needed to want to be holy. God's answer was to send God's Son, which did several important things. First, Jesus was full of grace. Jesus, fully God, willingly became a man and walked among humanity. By his obedience to his Father, he showed humility. He was compassionate and wise and suffered. He even allowed himself to be humiliated on the cross and die as a rejected criminal. His suffering proved he was meek and full of grace. He wanted to please God more than anything, more than life itself; that was his joy.

Second, God raised Jesus from the dead. Once Jesus was raised from the dead, any who honored Jesus were honored by his Father. Through faith in Christ, recognizing what Jesus did and who he was, God honored us. By loving and worshiping Jesus, God accepted us as one of God's children.

Third, faith in Jesus resulted in receiving the Holy Spirit. The Spirit is the source of grace. God's Spirit is the Spirit of Christ. Once we humble ourselves and surrender our lives to Jesus Christ, we are filled with God's grace. There is an explosion gifted by God (God's Spirit) of new desires and abilities to please God. Holiness becomes a passion and a joy. The tools we need to build a community are restored.

What God finds attractive in the believer is not perfection but hunger for perfection. It is like the enthusiastic, unskilled dancer who just wants to learn how to dance. He or she is not that coordinated; they dance poorly. But their enthusiasm for dance is so infectious that the dance instructor loves them. Think of King David in the Old Testament. He was such a flawed person, yet enthusiastic for God. David was a terrible dancer, but few have ever been more enthusiastic. God sees the "want" more than the

182

quality of the dance, and God accepts the believer based on their faith and passion, not so much their flawlessness. Grace works its magic, and our desire for worship and holiness endears God to us, the sinners. We are saved by faith in Christ; through grace, we become enthusiastic dancers.

God is not going to leave us as inadequate dancers. Grace continues its work in our lives. Once we come to Christ and experience an initial flood of grace—that is, energy for holiness—we continue to experience grace. Grace begins to shape us into what God wants us to be. Grace is a healing force and inspires virtues. Grace inspires gifts. Grace inspires skills to live holy lives. Grace inspires our vocation and shapes who God wants us to be. Grace changes us. Our will bends toward God's will, and through grace, we find joy in what we do. Living by grace is such a joy that we willingly suffer for Christ. Grace is freedom that comes from following our passions. Those passions are God-given, and they are so deep and powerful that they feel like our own passions.

Grace leads us in the dance of love. Grace shows us how to have a community of acceptance and belonging by changing our desires. It shows us how to love. Love is the dance, and its consequence is community and communion. Grace does not cause conformity, but uniqueness, creativity, and unity around Christ.

Humility is to grace as music is to dance. Humility activates grace. Our first encounter with grace is through faith in Jesus Christ, an act of surrender. Faith is proclaiming Jesus Christ as our Lord. We surrender to his lordship. We grow and mature by grace. We serve, forgive, and give; we are meek, poor in spirit, and even suffer. In all cases, these acts of humility result in a flood of transformative grace. Change comes from humility.

If we want to be better people, the key is to focus on humility. If, deep down, you want to dance but have no real clue how to dance, you will dance when the right music is played. The dance might not be pretty, but what dancing we do leads to better dancing. The music inspires dance. Humility opens our hearts and allows grace to flow in; humility inspires a passion for godliness. The first step we take to start our dance is surrender. We surrender our lives to Jesus Christ. The interaction of humility and grace causes a snowball effect. Righteousness develops and grows as we humble ourselves and practice grace-motivated righteousness. We change.

Grace can be minimized by bitterness. If we become angry with God or others, we can become embittered. Bitterness is what arises when we concentrate on an injustice we have suffered. We relive the injustice, and we replay in our minds what we should have said or done. We even tell others about the injustice we suffered. Bitterness obstructs the flow of grace. Adam and Eve were tempted, but their sin became resentment toward God. God was unjust, God had something they wanted, and God was keeping it from them. Adam and Eve lived in God's grace, but covetousness and the resulting bitterness led to sin. Pride became their nature, and their sins destroyed their communion and community. Hebrews 12:15 says that the root of bitterness will ruin a person. Nothing kills the passion for dancing like a good argument and the festering hurt afterward. The solution is forgiveness, an act of humility, which vanquishes bitterness.

Becoming Acceptable

Why the confusion about grace? Why was grace initially understood as a force of change and later demoted to a powerless status of being? Grace went from "I can" to "I am." This change in perspective produced the alleged duck analogy that the

Danish philosopher Soren Kierkegaard reportedly shared. The ducks waddled and lamented how powerless they were. They were slow, waddling ducks living in the mud of life. They attended church and heard about how they could fly. Then they waddled home. They never used their wings to fly. His point was the ducks had much more potential than they realized, and much of their suffering was because they ignored their potential. Grace as a force can be known and understood. The more we know and the more we understand, the greater its effect on our lives.

It is probably the case that the Reformation muddied the theological waters. The classical understanding of grace became hidden in conflict over the Roman Catholic Church's civil and religious control and excesses. The protesters left the Catholic Church and started their own churches. They were frustrated, threatened with imprisonment, and outspoken about almost all things Catholic. As a result, over time, there were two Protestant reactions to Christian standards of behavior. One reaction was to diminish the importance of good behavior and focus on acceptance. The focus on accepting others, it was thought, allowed one to achieve what he or she needed, which was to belong. In its extreme form, this approach led to universalism, the belief that all were accepted and saved.

However, as everyone knows, requiring everyone to accept unacceptable behavior makes forming a community impossible. The selfish do not practice love (and its virtues), which is the very foundation of community. In addition, the hostility Protestants felt about the Catholic Church clouded their theology. They focused on the Catholic Church's rituals, excesses, and dominance of others, and they lost sight of the teachings of grace as a force of change.

The other extreme of forming community that other Protestants promoted was to enforce requirements so that one could live in community. This tactic was like membership in an exclusive organization and living by the strict rules. This approach was legalistic. Each member of the community was obligated to conform in order to be in the community. Sadly, even John Calvin used this approach in his Genevan theocracy. He established rules of religious devotion that those in Geneva were expected to follow, and if they did not, the citizens were punished by imprisonment, torture, and even death.

This legalistic approach to community formation leads to the labeling of people as "insiders" and "outsiders." And this results in a community of pride, resentment, hypocrisy, abuses of power, and dominance. Communities of elites are popular because the elites receive honor. Jesus challenged the Pharisees not because they preached the law, but because they lived as elites (Luke 18:10-12). They were not humble servants. The majority, who are not among the elite, live on the margin outside of the community and feed the pride of the privileged. The problem with pietism is piety and its companion, pride.

These two perspectives are often seen in church history. Both extremes are trying to do the same thing. They are trying to form a community—one, with no behavioral boundaries, just acceptance; and the other, with strict behavioral boundaries that force all to conform. But grace does what neither extreme can do. Grace produces change so that we behave in ways such that we can be accepted. Yes, that is correct: grace makes us acceptable. Our grace-inspired behaviors allow us to form meaningful communities. There is no way to have a community where there is selfishness and pride. Grace gives the Christian a passion for a virtuous life, one that makes us likable.

Because grace leads to meaningful community, we can measure the effects of grace. When grace is successful, we form communities. Is grace changing us? Look at your community. Are you in a community? Is that community meaningful? Does that community reflect honor for the other, service to the other, and humility? The Holy Spirit birthed the church of Jesus Christ to be a community of worship and fellowship. And the Holy Spirit gives grace to the followers of Christ to make community possible.

It is easy to like a selfless person. It is easy to like a person who willingly and enthusiastically serves us. Rainbow World becomes a reality in the here and now as our grace-inspired behaviors help us achieve God's community. Our passion to be selfless and our selfless behaviors make us acceptable to our community. We belong because we have value, and our value is our humility and selflessness.

We dance because faith gives us grace—a passion for dancing. By dancing we find acceptance and belonging. And we cannot brag, for the dance we dance is God in us.

I Am Not Powerless Because I Want to Dance

The book of James, one of the oldest written books in the New Testament, talks about change. The writer does an amazing job of clearly explaining the need to change. In light of grace, his words make perfect sense. How can one say they have faith, yet there is no visible evidence of their faith? James says to show me you have changed by changing: "I will show you my faith by my works" (James 2:18). James later gives his readers assurance that God has placed God's Spirit within them, and that God's Spirit gives grace to the humble (James 4:5-6). We are not given an identity with no actions that demonstrate that identity. A dancer dances; a person who does not dance is not a dancer. We cannot call a person "changed" if he or she is not changing. Faith and change are inseparable. Where there is no change, there is no faith.

These expectations to change could leave one feeling hopeless, but James's reference to the Holy Spirit, humility, and grace makes change possible. The Spirit gives grace to the humble, and he or she can change. By faith in Christ and the infusion of grace, we find freedom and righteousness. By grace, the two are inseparable. By being changed, we find acceptance by God and by others. It is like children when they are small: their enthusiasm and energy to excel at reading, dance, soccer, swimming, or spelling gains their parent's admiration. They are not perfect, but their drive to be more than they are touches a parent's heart. We are acceptable by God because of our passion to change.

Do you want to change? Change is the result of grace, and grace is found in humility. Do men and women have a small role to play as far as changing? Yes—they must humble themselves, and then they receive grace. This understanding is why the words surrender, brokenness, repentance, submission, lordship, and servanthood are words found in the Bible. They are the keys to change. Humility is the opposite of working harder to change. Humility is surrender. Humility is recognition of how incapable we are of doing good or being good by our efforts. All the twelve-step addiction programs start with public confession and surrender. "I am an alcoholic. I am powerless to change. I cannot change alone." Theologians of old agree that humility and surrender are essential if we want to change.

When you read the scriptures, you realize that they are a menu of ideas about acts of humility. The Beatitudes and much of the Sermon on the Mount are litanies about acts of humility. The constant call by Jesus to his disciples to surrender and follow him, accept that they are sinners, be servants, and be the least if they want to be the greatest are all challenges to be humble. Jesus calls his disciples to the service of others and to humility. When our sins push us to the margins of society and, in our embarrassment, we surrender, our lives can change. God even gives grace to the humiliated. Humility starts God's grace. The Last Supper, where Jesus washed his disciples' feet, showed them the way. Jesus, God in the flesh, washed their feet.

All of these acts of service are talking about humility. We set our sails to catch the winds of change through humility. We change by grace, a wind that makes us feel freedom and inspires and motivates us to holiness and godliness. By the gift of grace, we dance because we want to dance.

Change is found in faith in Jesus Christ. Through faith in Christ, the believer is given their first dose of grace. Then grace—these new delights—open the believer to a life of delightful selflessness. Selflessness produces what we all need: a place of acceptance and belonging. The secret sauce to grace is humility. The Bible becomes our guide on how to love God and others. It is our map. It explains how to be humble and build community. God gives grace to replicate the community that God is.

What is grace? Grace is God in us making us willing and able to do His will. How do we change? By humility, God fills us with grace. What is the work of grace? Grace starts a virtuous life of selflessness that makes us acceptable in our community—we belong.

A Sinner's Prayer

God of creation and community, I confess that I am a sinner. I am broken by pride and selfishness. I profess that Jesus Christ, your Son, was humble and obedient and died on the cross to bring me hope. You, God, glorified your Son by raising him from the dead. I proclaim he is my Lord and want my life to glorify him. Fill me with your Spirit and transform me by your grace. Amen

Bibliography

Aquinas, Thomas. 1991. *Summa Theologia*. Translated by Timothy S McDermott. Allen, TX: Christian Classics.

Artemi, Eirini. 2017. "The Term Perichoresis from Cappadocian Fathers to Maximus Confessor." *International Journal of European Studies* 1 (1): 21–29.

Augustine. 2007. *Essential Sermons*. Edited by Boniface Ramsey. New York: New City Press Hyde Park.

———. 2010. *On Grace and Free Will*. Translated by Philip Schaff. Kindle. n.p.: GLH Publishing.

———. 2011. *On the Spirit and the Letter*. Translated by Philip Schaff. Kindle. n.p.: Beloved Publishing.

———. 2014. *On the Trinity*. Translated by Philip Schaff. Kindle. n.p.: Aeterna Press.

Barth, Karl, and Keith L Johnson. 2019. *The Essential Karl Barth: A Reader and Commentary*. Kindle. Grand Rapids, MI: Baker Academic.

Boehestein, William. 2014. "Thinking About Vocation." *Legionier Ministries* (blog). July 14, 2014. https://www.ligonier.org/blog/thinking-vocation.

Bonhoeffer, Dietrich. 1995. *The Cost of Discipleship*. 1st Touchstone ed. New York: Touchstone.

Bosch, David Jacobus. 2011. *Transforming Mission: Paradigm Shifts in Theology of Mission*. Twentieth anniversary ed, Kindle. American Society of Missiology Series, no. 16. Maryknoll, NY: Orbis Books.

Bouwsma, William J. 1988. *John Calvin: A Sixteenth-Century Portrait*. New York: Oxford University Press.

Calvin, John. 1509. *The Institutes of The Christian Religion*. Grand Rapids, MI: Christian Classics Ethereal Library. http://www.ccel.org/ccel/calvin/institutes.pdf?url=.

Carder, Kenneth L. 2016. "A Wesleyan Understanding of Grace." United Methodist Church, Interpreter. https://www.resourceumc.org/en/content/a-wesleyan-understanding-of-grace.

Cavanaugh, William T. 1998. *Torture and Eucharist: Theology, Politics, and the Body of Christ*. 1st edition. Malden, MA: Wiley-Blackwell.

Cheah, Fook Ming. 1995. "A Review of Luther and Erasmus: Free Will and Salvation." *Protestant Reformed Theological Journal* 29 (1). www.prca.org.org/prtj/nov95b.

Chester, Tim. 2005. *Delighting in the Trinity*. Kindle. Grand Rapids, MI: Monarch Books.

"Confession of Faith and Government for Cumberland Presbyterians." 1984. Cumberland Presbyterian Church. Memphis, TN. http://www.cumberland.org/gao/confession.

Corey, Benjamin. 2016. "Blessed Are The Shalom-Makers: Toward a Shalom Focused Human Trafficking Aftercare Social Movement." Pasadena, CA: Fuller Theological Seminary.

Dodds, Adam. 2017. *The Mission of The Triune God: Trinitarian Missiology in The Tradition of Lesslie Newbigin*. Kindle. Eugene, OR: Pickwick Publications.

Ford, Paul Richard. 1998. *Discovering Your Ministry Identity: For Teams, Groups, or Individuals : Learning to Be Who You Already Are*. n.p.: ChurchSmart Resources.

Friedrich, Gerhard, and Gerhard Kittel, eds. 1968. *Theological Dictionary of the New Testament Vol. 6*. Vol. VI. Grand Rapids, MI: Eerdmans.

Gaillardetz, Richard R. 2008. *Ecclesiology for a Global Church: A People Called and Sent*. Theology in Global Perspective. Maryknoll, NY: Orbis Books.

Graham, Billy. 1997. *Just as I Am: The Autobiography of Billy Graham*. 1st ed. San Francisco, CA: HarperSanFrancisco; Zondervan.

Haight, Roger. 1979. *The Experience and Language of Grace*. New York: Paulist Press.

Hardon, John A. 1981. *The Catholic Catechism*. Garden City, NY.: Doubleday.

Healy, Nicholas M. 2014. "The Christian Life: In Addition to Augustine and Aquinas." *New Blackfriars* 95 (1056): 234–46. https://doi.org/10.1111/nbfr.12065.

Henry, Matthew. 1822. *A Discourse Concerning Meekness and Quietness of Spirit*. Glasgow: D. MacKenzie.

James, William. 2011. *The Varieties of Religious Experience*. Digital version. New York, NY: Logmans, Green and Co. http://search.ebscohost.com.

Johnson, Darrell W. 2002. *Experiencing the Trinity*. Kindle. Vancouver: Regent College Pub.

Kennedy, D. 1912. "Sacraments." In *The Catholic Encylopedia*. New York: Robert Appleton Company. http://www.newadvent.org/cathen/13295a.htm.

Kim, Van Nam. 2014. *Multicultural Theology and New Evangelization*. Lanham, MD: University Press of America, Inc.

Kittel, Gerhard, and Geoffrey William Bromiley. 1964. *Theological Dictionary of the New Testament. Vol. 2*. Grand Rapids, MI: Wm. B. Eerdmans.

Kittel, Gerhard, and Gerhard Friedrich, eds. 1972. *Theological Dictionary of the New Testament Vol. 8*. Vol. VIII. Grand Rapids, MI: Eerdmans.

———, eds. 1974. *Theological Dictionary of the New Testament. Vol. 9*. Translated by Geoffrey Bromiley. Vol. IX. Grand Rapids, MI: Eerdmans.

Knight, Henry H. 2018. *John Wesley: Optimist of Grace*. Cascade Companions 32. Eugene, OR: Cascade Books.

Kolakowski, Leszek. 2012. *God Owes Us Nothing: A Brief Remark on Pascal's Religion and on the Spirit of Jansenism*. Ebook. Chicago: The University of Chicago Press.

Kotter, John P. 2012. *Leading Change*. Kindle. Boston, MA: Harvard Business Review Press.

Lewis, C. S. 2001. *Mere Christianity*. 1st HarperCollins ed. San Francisco: HarperSanFrancisco.

Lewis, Gordon R., and Bruce A. Demarest. 1996. *Integrative Theology*. Grand Rapids, MI: Zondervan.

Luther, Martin. 1520. *Concerning Christian Liberty*. Kindle. n.p.: Astounding-Stories.

———. 2018. *The Bondage of the Will, Luther's Reply to Erasmus' on Free Will*. Translated by Henry Cole. Kindle. n.p.: e-artnow.

McGrath, Alister E., ed. 1995. *The Christian Theology Reader*. Reprint. Oxford: Blackwell.

Minor, Vernon Hyde. 2016. *Baroque Visual Rhetoric*. Toronto Italian Studies. Toronto: University of Toronto Press.

Moreau, A. Scott, Susan Greener, and Evvy Hay Campbell. 2014. *Effective Intercultural Communication (Encountering Mission): A Christian Perspective*. Kindle edition. Grand Rapids, MI: Baker Academic.

Nee, Watchman. 1972. *The Latent Power of the Soul*. New York: Christian Fellowship Publishers.

Nieuwenhove, Rik Van, and Joseph Wawrykow. 2010. "Grace." In *The Theology of Thomas Aquinas*, Kindle (PDF). Notre Dame, IN: University of Notre Dame Press.

O'Callaghan, Paul. 2016. *Children of God in the World: An Introduction to Theological Anthropology*. Washington, D.C.: The Catholic University of America Press.

Ott, Craig, Stephen J. Strauss, and Timothy C. Tennent. 2010. *Encountering Theology of Mission: Biblical Foundations, Historical Developments, and Contemporary Issues*. Grand Rapids, MI: Baker Academic.

Paredes, Melissa. 2015. "7 Tips to Find God's Will for Your Life." Wycliffe Bible Translators. www.wycliffe.org. October 30, 2015. https://www.wycliffe.org/blog/posts/7-tips-to-find-gods-will-for-your-life.

Payton, James R. 2007. *Light from the Christian East: An Introduction to the Orthodox Tradition*. Downers Grove, IL: IVP Academic.

Pohle, J. 1909b. "Actual Grace." In *The Catholic Encyclopedia*. New York: Robert Appleton Company. http://www.newadvent.org/cathen/06689x.htm.

———. 1909a. "Sanctifying Grace." In *The Catholic Encylopedia*. New York: New Advent. http://www.newadvent.org/cathen/06701a.htm.

Rahner, Karl. 1961. *Theological Investigations*. Translated by Cornelius Ernst. Vol. I. London: Helicon Press.

———. 1997. *The Trinity*. New York: Crossroad Pub.

Scazzero, Peter. 2017. *Emotionally Healthy Spirituality: It's Impossible to Be Spiritually Mature, While Remaining Emotionally Immature*. Kindle Updated edition. Grand Rapids, MI: Zondervan.

Segundo, Juan Luis. 1973. *Grace and The Human Condition*. Vol. 2. A Theology for Artisans of a New Humanity. Maryknoll, NY: Orbis Books.

Smith, James. 1837. *The Posthumos Works of The Reverand and Pious James M'Gready, Late Minister of The Gospel, in Henderson, KY*. Nashville, TN: J. Smith's Steam Press.

Sproul, R.C. 2005. "Augustine and Pelagius." LeaderU. December 12, 2005. http://www.leaderu.com/theology/augpelagius.html.

Swindoll, Charles R. 1990. *The Grace Awakening*. Dallas: Word Pub.

Tanck, Brian. 2021. "OptIN, A Way of Life." Presented at the OptIN Leader Orientation, Scottsboro, AL, September 23.

Tanck, Micaiah, and Tanck, Brian. 2020. *OptIN, Rituals That Lead to Encounter*. Scottsboro, AL: Self-Published, Scottsboro Cumberland Presbyterian Church.

Thomas, Lynndon. 2020. *Relational Missions, Concepts, Perspectives, and Practices That Inform Global Missions*. 1st ed. Memphis, TN: Ministry Council of the Cumberland Presbyterian Church.

Vanderschaaf, Mark. 1976. "Predestination and Certainty of Salvation in Augustine and Calvin." *Studies in Historical Theology and Ethics* 30 (1).
https://repository.westernsem.edu/pkp/index.php/rr/article/download/774/807.

Wesley, John. 2013. *The Complete Sermons: John Wesley*. Kindle. n.p.: Hargreaves Publishing.

Westminister Confession of Faith. 1647. PDF digital.
https://www.opc.org/documents/CFLayout.pdf.

Winter, Ralph D., Steven C. Hawthorne, Darrell R. Dorr, D. Bruce Graham, and Bruce A. Koch, eds. 2009. *Perspectives on the World Christian Movement: A Reader*. 4th ed. Pasadena, CA: William Carey Library.